The Quilters' Guild Collection

Contemporary Quilts, Heritage Inspiration

The Quilters' Guild of the British Isles

EDITED BY BRIDGET LONG

Bridget Long

Dawn Thomas

David and Charles

First published in the UK in 2005 by
David & Charles
Brunel House   Newton Abbot   Devon
www.davidandcharles.co.uk
David & Charles is a subsidiary of F+W (UK) Ltd.,
an F+W Publications Inc. company

A catalogue record for this book is available from the British Library.

ISBN 0 7153 1816 0

Paperback edition published in North America in 2005 by
KP Books, an F+W Publications Inc. company
700 East State Street, Iola, WI 54990
715-445-2214/888-457-2873
www.krause.com

A catalog record for this book is available from the Library
of Congress: 2004098439

ISBN 0-89689-185-2

Photography by Karl Adamson and Simon Whitmore
Printed in China by Sun Fung Offset Binding Co., Ltd.
Commissioning editor   Vivienne Wells
Desk editor   Ame Verso
Project editor   Karen Hemingway
Executive art editor   Ali Myer
Senior designer   Lisa Wyman
Production controller   Ros Napper

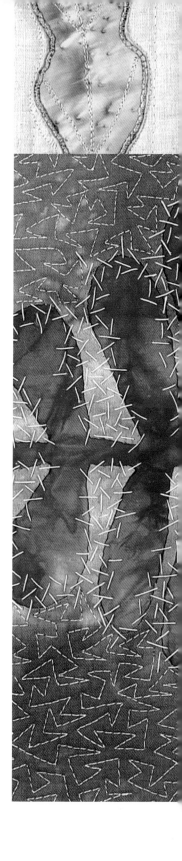

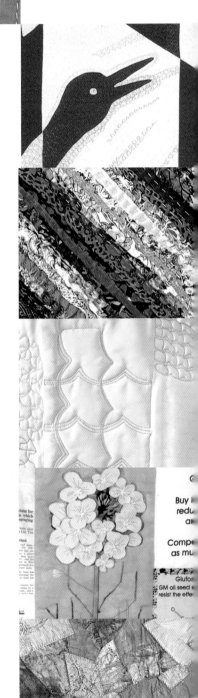

CONTENTS

FOREWORD

The traditions of British quiltmaking go back centuries, through the thousands of anonymous quilters who have contributed to the varied techniques, styles and patterns. The aim of this book is to look back on this heritage (through quilts in The Quilters' Guild Collection) to enrich our quiltmaking future.

The Quilters' Guild is delighted to encourage quilters to develop their design skills, guided by the 12 outstanding teachers who have contributed to this book. We are grateful to these inspirational quilters for sharing their skills and knowledge, and to Bridget Long, for her excellent work throughout on planning, administering, co-ordinating and writing this book.

Finally, we should record the debt we owe members and staff who were instrumental in establishing and building the wonderful collection of quilts now owned by The Quilters' Guild. Without the hours they spent caring for those quilts, this book would not have been possible.

Fay Allwood
President, The Quilters' Guild of the British Isles, 2003–2005

INTRODUCTION

For today's quiltmakers, the work of the past can be seen as a vast resource for creating new work. The influential contemporary British quilter, Pauline Burbidge once said, 'I don't want to just throw off the traditions of quiltmaking, because I am close to that tradition and love being inspired by it. I am certainly inspired by the old quilts and like to show that inspiration through my work'.[1]

By recognizing the rich resource of British quilts and drawing on their distinctive characteristics, modern quilters can develop new and challenging designs for the future. Following that path, 12 contemporary quilters have taken inspiration from specific styles of quilt held in The Quilters' Guild museum collection to make their own very individual quilts for this book. To place them in their context, details of British quilt history accompany the quilts, with references to take the topics further.

Inspiration for Design

Many talented quilters may be frightened by the thought of design, assuming that leading quilters are somehow able to pluck designs out of the air. The 12 quilters featured in this book demonstrate that by following tried and trusted processes and routines, a quilt design can be developed from any object used for inspiration. The 12 projects show how varied the approaches can be, from drawing grids with pencil and paper or making paper collages, to using design software on

The House Blocks Quilt, *188 x 236cm (74 x 93in)*,
The Quilters' Guild's first acquisition in 1979

a computer. The routines are explained and illustrated and, if experimented with, could give anyone the confidence to take a further step down the designing route. The featured designers' favourite techniques for dyeing or texturing cloth will help quiltmakers give their work even more individuality.

Many of the 12 quilters acknowledge that drawing is not their forte, so they follow design processes that do not need that skill. One even resorts to a computer to do the drawing work. All, however, are constantly keeping their eyes open for new things that intrigue and fascinate, spending time recording what they see. A lesson that any aspiring designer will take away from this book is the need to observe, collect and record. Collections of printed ephemera, found objects and photographs as well as drawings and sketches can be stored in an ideas book or file. Whilst some of the sketchbooks shown here are works of art in their own right, the basic principle to collect for inspiration can be applied to a simple file as well as a sketchbook.

Selection of sketchbooks from the contributing quilters

The Quilters' Guild and its Collections

The Quilters' Guild of the British Isles was formed in 1979 and is a national organization promoting quiltmaking across the United Kingdom. The Quilters' Guild aims to give quiltmaking the status it deserves both as a craft and as an art, and to encourage and maintain a high standard of workmanship and design. As a registered educational charity, The Quilters' Guild works to promote the appreciation, knowledge and understanding of the heritage, art and techniques of quiltmaking.

In the first few years of The Quilters' Guild's existence, a number of quilts and items of clothing were donated to form a small collection, which was used as study material for members. The first quilt was the House Blocks Quilt, consisting of blocks made by members of a previous organization, The Quilt Circle, including influential quilters and teachers such as Deirdre and Jean Amsden. The blocks were raffled and won by Jean, who made them into a quilt and donated it to the newly formed Quilters' Guild in 1979.

The growth of the collection was slow and unplanned, with only 18 items after five years. In 1990, The Quilters' Guild initiated a project documenting pre-1960s privately owned quilts and other items and the results of the British Quilt Heritage Project were published in 1995.[2] The book

marked a time when there was a growth in interest in British quilt history and, perhaps due to the raised profile of The Quilters' Guild, there was a rapid growth in the quilt collection, which has continued to the present day. The Quilters' Guild achieved full museum registration for its collection in 2001.

The collection now has over 450 large items, ranging from the oldest known dated patchwork to contemporary quilts commissioned from internationally and nationally known British quilt artists. The Quilters' Guild has a national collecting policy, collecting quilts and related items from across the British Isles to represent a broad range of styles, techniques and regional influences up to the present day. Striking quilts, clothing and domestic items from the 18th, 19th and 20th centuries are stored alongside tools, templates and fabrics. The need to collect the mundane as well as the wonderful is acknowledged, so recent acquisitions have included modern clothing in patchwork and quilting – and even a blue nylon quilted dressing gown.

Bridget Long

Up the Stairs, *100 x 100cm (39 x 39in)*, commissioned by Region 13 of The Quilters' Guild and made by Elizabeth Brimelow in 2004. Donated to the collection of contemporary quilts, celebrating 25 years of The Quilters' Guild

400 YEARS OF QUILTS

Four hundred years ago, people in Britain lived in a world of plain cloth. For the majority of them, the textiles available for clothing and furnishing were wool, linen, silk and the bast fibres such as hemp. All of these were available in plain colours because, although European textile manufacturers were skilled dyers and weavers, they lacked extensive skills to print pattern on cloth. Decorative weave silks were produced but, being expensive, were accessible only to the wealthier members of society. For centuries in Britain there had been a flowering of needlework and embroidery skills, which were used both in professional workshops and the domestic environment. People were able to use a variety of techniques such as fabric manipulation, punching, slashing, embroidery, quilting and inevitably probably patchwork to add pattern and texture to cloth in order to decorate their plain world.

Detail of the centre of the 1718 Silk Patchwork Coverlet

1718 Silk Patchwork Coverlet

The earliest known patchwork that bears a date is a silk patchwork coverlet dated 1718. Measuring 169 x 185cm (66½ x 73in), the 1718 Silk Patchwork Coverlet (opposite) consists of 182 figurative, geometric and decorative blocks of various sizes; the basic and smallest block size is 11 x 11cm (4½ x 4½in). In the central area of the upper half of the coverlet is a basic unit with the pieced date and initials 'E' and 'H' placed below a heart block and above figures of a man and woman with further heart motif blocks.

The whole coverlet has been pieced using paper templates. The fabric is wrapped over the templates and is tacked (basted) through the seam allowance and paper only, thus avoiding sewing through the top layer of silk. The pieces are joined together with fine hand oversewing (whip stitch) to create the blocks, which are then assembled in a complex grid design incorporating the various sizes of blocks. The paper templates have been left in place.

The entire coverlet is a tour de force of stitching. The individual blocks are often complex designs of figures, animals, birds and flowers made from a number of complicated shapes that require skilled hands to be sewn accurately and neatly. Many of the more difficult blocks are of the base unit size, which makes the individual components or pieces very small. To add to the complexity, the background behind many of the figurative blocks is diagonally quartered in contrasting fabrics, creating extra pieces for each block design.[1,2] The only embroidery used in the entire quilt is for the eyes of the animals.

The coverlet is laid out like a sampler and is patterned with motifs of domesticated animals and birds together with game such as deer, pheasants and partridges, reflecting the rural life of the family who owned it. It has passed through generations of farming gentry in Wiltshire but, sadly, extensive research has not revealed the owner(s) of the initials EH.[3] The fabrics, all of silk with the exception of a few pieces of wool/silk, wool/linen and silk/linen mix, appear to be almost all dress fabrics and many, dating from the 17th century, show signs of previous use.

1718 Silk Patchwork Coverlet, 169 x 185cm (66½ x 73in)

Detail from the 1718 Silk Patchwork Coverlet

this time. It is a misfortune that no earlier examples have survived. The survivors demonstrate the popularity of the half-square triangle shape in patchwork, used in diagonally quartered blocks or square on point designs. This simple shape continued to be seen extensively in silk patchwork right through the 18th century.

Texture on Plain Cloth

In the 18th century, quilting continued to be used for bedcovers and garments as before. Professional workshops supplied fashionable wadded and corded quilted items in silk and linen, whilst imported cotton quilting from Marseilles, France and India could be purchased from British shops. This trade was supplying the wealthier end of the market in which ornate textural quilted patterns were desirable for both furnishing and clothing.

The 18th-century fashion for dresses with an open front showing a petticoat, fed the trade in wadded silk petticoats to be bought off the peg or to order. The green silk petticoat shown below and containing the standard quilting patterns of flowers with wave motifs and zigzags seen on such 'mass-produced' garments, is typical of the styles available.[6]

The silk fabrics show that the owners had relatively high status, representing the merchant class, although the fabrics were not the best of the day. Only a few show flat metal strips, probably silver, woven as weft stripes in the silk; an indication of the costly cloth purchased and used by the wealthy classes.[4]

The 1718 Silk Patchwork Coverlet has been compared with a small number of other surviving silk patchwork items from the early 18th century, including a coverlet dated 1726 that is held in the collections of the McCord Museum of Canadian History, Montreal, Canada and came to Canada from Norwich, England.[5] All the items show a confidence in technique that would suggest that patchwork was widely known and used at

Utilitarian bedcovers and garments, incorporating basic quilting and patchwork, were likely to be made at the same time to provide both warmth and decoration. Sadly, evidence from this period does not exist for quilting activity in the lower social classes because the items would probably have been used to destruction rather than being stored away for future generations to find.

Silk quilted petticoat from the 18th century

The Blossoming of Patchwork

In 1609 William Finch, a far-sighted employee of the East India Company, suggested buying Indian-produced cloth such as muslins, pintadoes and quilts for sale in Britain. He was able to appreciate that the textile makers of India had achieved great skills in spinning and printing cottons, producing a cloth that would be a novelty in Europe.

Printed Indian cottons such as chintzes had an exotic look, provided by the large-scale flowing floral designs incorporating printed and painted motifs in strong red, blue, yellow, purple, black and orange, which the home textile manufacturers could not match. At first wealthier classes were reluctant to buy Indian cloth, although Samuel Pepys, the diarist bought a chintz dress for his wife in 1663 and had an informal robe for himself. However, by the end of the 17th century, wealthier ladies would wear chintz for upper garments as daywear, as well as undergarments, and chintz was used for bedcovers and wall hangings, thus establishing its fashionable status.

European linen and wool manufacturers saw the imported cottons as a threat and campaigned for a control and then a ban of imports, which many countries, including Britain, imposed in the late 1600s and early 1700s. Restrictions on the import of Indian cotton continued until 1774, although loopholes in the bans and illegal importation of cloth allowed Indian chintzes to be widely available throughout the century.

The famous Levens Hall, Cumbria patchwork quilt and bed curtain are made from imported Indian chintzes in an unembellished interlocking design of octagons, crosses, long hexagons and rectangles. Claimed by the family to be made in about 1708, the items are unlike the silk patchwork from the early 18th century, such as the 1718 Silk Patchwork Coverlet. Recent research has been unable to confirm the date, but the

Detail of plate print quilt from the late 18th century, owned by the Bell family of Kendal

Levens Hall pieces can still be regarded as the earliest patchwork made from printed cotton.[7]

European textile manufacturers faced with the threat of a desirable, novel product finally had to compete by developing printing skills on both linen and cotton and a home-based printing industry grew throughout the 18th century. As printed cotton and linen became available from European production, it was incorporated into patchwork. Rare survivors have been recorded from the mid-18th century such as the Clamshell patchwork bed hangings containing both Indian and European printed and painted cottons in the Victoria and Albert Museum, London.[8]

Towards the end of the century, cottons printed from wooden blocks (block prints) and from engraved copper plates (plate prints) were readily available but expensive and highly fashionable for both furnishing and dress. The detail of a late 18th-century wholecloth quilt, owned by the Bell family from Kendal (left), shows a plate print linen with a trellis of fine flowing flower stems with larger finely drawn flowers such as passionflowers, pinks and roses. It is quilted in double-lined Clamshell and Wineglass.

Cotton patchwork was a fashionable needlework technique and surviving examples are often intricate designs made by ladies who had access to many fabrics, possessed needlework and art design skills, and had time available to create complex patchwork, using the time-consuming technique of piecing over papers. Both the complex frame coverlet containing fabric from the 1795–1805 period (see pages 11 and 32) and the Mariner's Compass Coverlet (page 10) of a slightly later date are typical examples of the patchwork being produced. These items are very often unquilted coverlets rather than quilts, suggesting they were more for show than for functional bedcovers. The Mariner's

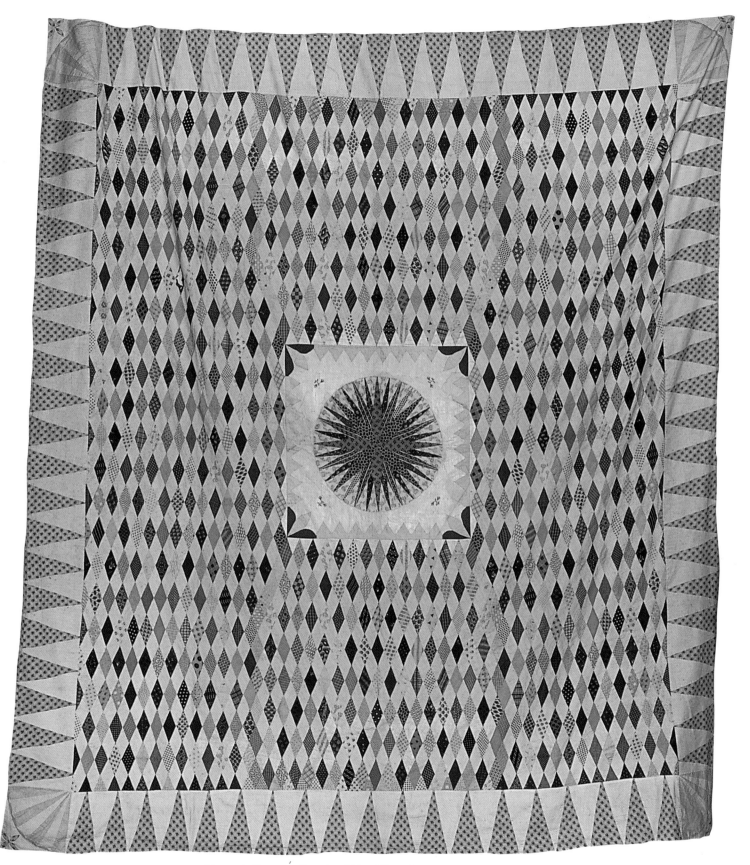

Mariner's Compass Coverlet, 252 x 273cm (99 x 108in), a pieced coverlet
with a compass pattern centre from the early 19th century

Compass Coverlet (opposite) has a very complex compass pattern pieced centre and is surrounded by diamonds of printed cottons and linens alternating with plain and dimity (containing a textural weave) cotton.

Panels block printed on to fabric lengths were cut and sold for use in patchwork or for cushions (pillows) and fire screens. They were often produced to commemorate important events such as George III's Golden Jubilee in 1810, Wellington's victory at Waterloo in 1815, or the wedding of Princess Charlotte of Wales and Leopold Prince of Saxe Coburg in 1816. Others were pleasing designs incorporating flowers, birds, baskets and figures such as the unused panel of feeding birds in a nest shown on the right and the eight panels in the quilt on page 13.

right Block-printed panel c. 1820

Detail of complex frame coverlet of 1795–1805

The Influence of Technology

In the early 19th century, technological developments were influencing the production techniques for printing cotton. Until then, printed cotton was aimed at the quality end of the market on the basis of cost. Block printing is a very time-consuming process involving a separate carved wooden block for each colour used in the design. Producing detailed, high-quality single colour with white designs, plate printing from engraved copper plates was also expensive because of the high cost of creating the plates.

In 1783, Thomas Bell of Glasgow developed a technique of engraved cylinder printing (printing using a metal roller), allowing the production of continuous lengths of printed cloth. Although not used until the 19th century, the roller-printing process allowed the development of new print styles that could not be achieved by the other two print processes and this, coupled with lower production costs, saw the popularity of printed cotton grow. Through the first decades of the century, the patterns became more and more complex as printers developed their skills of manipulating printing methods and dyeing techniques.

The growth of cotton production is reflected in the quilts and coverlets seen in the first half of the 19th century. No longer just the province of leisured ladies, cotton patchwork quilts were widely made as cotton became cheaper and more abundant. The quilts at this time were often simpler in design, most being made in an all-over mosaic or a frame style,

Detail of the centre of the frame quilt dated 1844;
the appliqué probably dates from the 1820s

reflecting the possible lack of artistic or drafting skills or even the time available to devote to the needlework. Patchwork was no longer mainly pieced over paper template shapes; the technique of seaming patchwork pieces with a running stitch was also used. Typical of the quilts made, the colourful frame quilt shown opposite is signed in the centre, 'JH Thorne September 3 1824', and is a mix of roller and block-printed dress cottons pieced in simple squares and rectangles. At its centre and on one of the outer frames are block-printed panels with a gothic ruin and flowers. It is heavily quilted in a frame design unrelated to the frame patchwork pattern.[9]

Patchwork was often quilted at this time, but the quilting layout tends to be unrelated to the pieced design. All-over quilting patterns such as Clamshell or straight lines in a zigzag were used, but the centre and frame-quilting layout with defined borders was common throughout the first half of the 19th century as seen in the Cockburn wholecloth quilt (see page 78).

Unlike Broderie Perse appliqué, which relied on printed motifs to provide the design, appliqué became more creative with individual designs often in a naïve style as seen in the centre of the frame quilt shown above. Dated 1844, the delightful appliqué centre, showing birds sitting on a rudimentary tree in a pot, was likely to have been made in the mid-1820s. It was probably finished with fabrics printed later, when the outer block design was added in the 1840s.

Frame quilt, *246 x 292cm (97 x 115in),* inscribed 'JH Thorne September 3 1824'

above Detail of Painted Silks Hexagon Coverlet,
112 x 163cm (44 x 64in), from the late 19th century

above Detail of pieced strippy quilt, *243 x 234cm
(95½ x 92in)*, from 1880–1900 in cotton and wool

Fashion and Utility

The different styles of quilt made in the second half of the 19th century are exemplified by the two pieces illustrated in detail here. Measuring 112 x 163cm (44 x 64in), the small coverlet or cover (left) is made from a variety of colourful, patterned silk hexagon rosettes set very effectively against a black silk hexagon background. The white centre to each rosette shows a small hand-painted flower. It has a border of silk diamonds with applied cords and braids and a deep multicoloured fringed border.

The dark-coloured quilt (below, left) with deep purple plain strips dividing pieced squares on point, contains a mix of wools and cottons. Made around 1880–1900 in the north east of England, it is a large bed quilt measuring 243 x 234cm (95½ x 92in) and is strip quilted with Cable border patterns and rose motifs on the squares. The quilt is very striking but simply made with many joined fabrics in the squares and an uneven shape to the finished piece.

The two pieces come from different worlds. The small silk coverlet was sewn by someone with access to luxury fabrics, who could afford to use cords, braids and fringes for ornament. The hexagons and diamonds are hand pieced over paper templates and the painted flowers are painstakingly worked. The cover is a showy piece made by a needlewoman with time to spend on patchwork, living in a stylishly furnished house where the cover would be on display. The pieced strippy quilt provided warmth for a bed and was made from the fabrics that were readily available to the quiltmaker. It is part of a tradition of patchwork and quilting in an area where finances are likely to have restricted the time spent quilting and the choice of fabrics used.

This split in quilt styles was led in part by a further revolution in textile production. In 1856, WH Perkin discovered the first synthetic dye from coal tar – a bright purple called 'mauveine'. Perkin's mauve was followed very quickly by other new aniline dyes, which were far more suitable for use on protein fibres such as silks and wools, rather than cotton. Throughout the century, printed cottons had moved down the social scale as they became cheaper. As the status of cotton declined, so silk again became more important. The novelty of the new bright coloured dyes on silks led to their predominance in fashion, especially in the last quarter of the 19th century. The silks were used for many

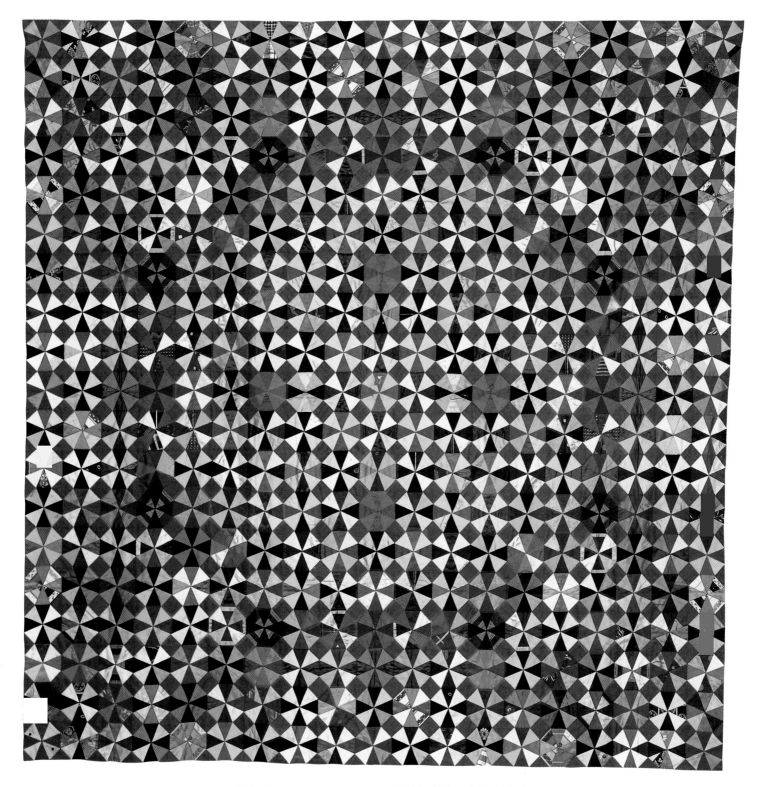

Kaleidoscope pattern mosaic quilt, *216 x 220cm (85 x 86½in)*,
made in silk by Elizabeth Watson of Cumbria in the late 19th century

Medallion Crazy Coverlet, 200 x 213cm (79 x 84in), made in silk and velvet by Frances Maria Fletcher (née Cope) for her wedding in 1873

was some resentment amongst the sisters who remained on the farm, especially as they had a new dress only once a year, made from a practical fabric of sombre colour.

Cotton quilts made at this time often testify to the thrift of the maker. Quilts were often simple in design, relying on quilting on large areas of plain fabric to provide the textural interest. Fabrics were frequently the widely available household cottons such as Turkey Red and white cottons seen in the Red and White Quilt (see page 38); many were recycled and, if purchased, were often obtained cheaply as fents or discarded sample books.

The simple cotton frame quilt seen opposite has four pieced borders of rectangles, the shape typical of sample books, showing many similar cotton print designs including some with different colourways. The centre of this quilt is an octagon containing larger pieces of furnishing cotton, some patterned with Art Nouveau inspired motifs. Cottons seen in quilts at this time have been mass-produced with repetitive often unoriginal designs. Influences such as the Art and Crafts Movement or Art Nouveau are not often seen in the patterns on cotton fabric for this type of market.

Simple cotton fabrics were often used for group projects, producing quilts as gifts or for fundraising. Bazaar quilts, usually two-coloured red and white or blue and white, raised money for church or chapel funds through the sale of patches in a quilt. The pieces were signed by the purchaser and embroidered before being incorporated into the quilt.

patchwork pieces during this time, as can be seen with the Irish Crazy Patchwork Coverlet (see page 71) and the Jubilee Quilt (see page 72), the Silk Triangles Coverlet (see page 90) and the Silk Log Cabin Table Cover (see page 46).

Three Watson sisters lived on a large farm in Cumbria at the end of the 19th century. After getting up at 5.00am to do their chores, they spent time sewing during daylight hours, particularly after lunch. They were prolific quilters, making both utilitarian quilts for the farm workers and finer pieces such as the dazzling silk Kaleidoscope pattern mosaic quilt shown on page 15, made by Elizabeth Watson for her 'bottom drawer' (although she never married).

Francis Maria Fletcher (née Cope) made the diamond, star and crazy coverlet shown above before her wedding in 1873, when she lived on a farm in Belper, Derbyshire. It is likely that she sourced the silk and velvets for the coverlet from her sister who was a buyer for a London fashion house and probably had access to fashionable fabrics. The family story is that there

Detail of signature quilt from Jarrow on Tyne made in 1897, made to celebrate Queen Victoria's Diamond Jubilee

Frame quilt, *222 x 235cm (87 x 93in)*, from the late 19th century, in cotton including samples

The white, blue and red cotton quilt bearing an embroidered portrait of Queen Victoria (left) in her Diamond Jubilee year in 1897, was made in Tyneside. Measuring 222cm (87in) square, it is inscribed 'Primitive Methodist Connexion Jarrow on Tyne Circuit' above and '1837 Diamond Jubilee 1897' below the portrait. The quilt features over 210 embroidered names including TT Harvey Circuit Steward and the Reverends C Seaman, J Atkinson and C Phillipson.It is unknown whether the quilt was made just in commemoration of the Jubilee or also to raise funds for the Methodist Church.

A Distinctive Style

The striking quilt shown opposite is simply made from plain wool. The harmonious use of strong deep colours, a simple patchwork frame design with a star in the centre and deeply incised quilting set off by the multicoloured prairie point edge are combined in a very pleasing effect.

Thought to have been made by Mrs Megan Jones at the end of the 19th or beginning of the 20th century, this quilt has a simple patchwork design enhanced by a centre and defined frame quilting layout that is typical of Welsh quilts of the period. In the first half of the 19th century, the centre and defined frame layout was ubiquitous, being used across the whole country. Welsh quilts continued to be quilted in this style, but in the north of England, quilt designers influenced the development of a much looser undefined frame style in the second half of the 19th century (see page 77).

The layout here consists of a large circle enclosed in a central square. The surrounding borders are separated by lines (defined) and contain quilt motifs such as leaves, spirals, four-petal flowers and pairs of Welsh Scissors. Welsh quilting motifs have a distinct character which, when combined with a defined framed layout, provide clues as to the likely provenance of the quilt.

The classic Welsh quilting layout can be seen in the bright blue wool and yellow cotton strippy (left). This also contains traditional quilting motifs such as a Wheel, Fans, Church Windows and spirals. Unlike strippies from the north of England (see page 101), Welsh strippies do not commonly have a strippy quilting pattern. The defined framed style is also seen in the two later quilts made for Claridges Hotel (see pages 22 and 23). Welsh quilts of the 20th century, made under the Rural Industries Bureau scheme, tend to have very precisely drafted patterns and accurately drawn framed layouts, indicating the high standards expected under the scheme, but they perhaps do not have the attraction of the more individual quilts made before that time.

Welsh strippy quilt, *195 x 213cm (77 x 84in)*, from the early 20th century

Welsh wool frame quilt, *198 x 204cm (78 x 80in),*
from the 19th or the beginning of the 20th century

Decline and Revival in the 20th Century

During the first two decades of the 20th century, the impact of World War I and changes in fashion affecting domestic textiles led to a decline in quiltmaking. Commercially produced woven cotton covers, machine-made 'Marcella' quilts, wool coverlets and eiderdowns were popular alternatives for beds. However, there was still a need for warm bedcovers, as demonstrated by the unusual and striking yellow and white quilt shown opposite, which is unwashed so it still has the blue pencil markings probably made by a quilt designer. It is likely to have been made in around 1910 in the Castleside area of County Durham, northern England. The quilting motifs along the large central diagonal cross shapes and the borders are well-known strippy/border designs, including Weardale Chain, Cable Twist and Plait, together with roses, freehand feathers and scrolling.

The rectangular red and white Star quilt shown right is from the same period, but its provenance is unknown. It varies from the standard square Star design attributed to Elizabeth Sanderson, with the central pieced star floating in a wide central rectangle and a reduced number of borders.

At this time, quilts were often made by itinerant quilters who worked for a daily rate, including food and lodging.[10] More were supplied by village quilters or from quilt clubs. Quiltmaking tended to be concentrated in only a few areas of Britain, particularly South Wales and the north east of England. In the industrial and mining areas in both these regions, quilt clubs operated as a regular source of income for families in straitened circumstances.[11, 12] The clubs had regular customers who paid for their quilts by subscription over a number of weeks. Quilts were delivered to the club members in turn and lots were often drawn for the order in which they were to be delivered. The quilter made a profit of about £1 to £1.10s (£1.50) on each quilt.[13]

In the late 1920s and 1930s, there was a determined effort by a number of organizations to revive quilting as a way of providing income for families. The Rural Industries Bureau worked with Mavis FitzRandolph to regenerate the quilting tradition in both South Wales and the north of England, drawing on the skills of existing quilters and establishing classes for new workers. Quilts, cushions (pillows), dressing gowns and bed jackets were made to order and were often sold through London shops such as the Little Gallery run by Muriel Rose.[14] A famous order was placed by Claridges Hotel, London for quilts and pillowslips for rooms in their new Art Deco style extension. Fifty quilters from South Wales and County Durham were involved in completing the order, some groups making a pair of large quilts with pillow covers to match in only one week.[15] The two well-used quilts seen on pages 22 and 23 (both made in South Wales) are survivors of this large order; they were rediscovered by the hotel in 1980 and donated to The Quilters' Guild. The peach coloured quilt reversing to blue is quilted in a classic Welsh centre and defined borders layout, with typical Welsh motifs. The cream quilt seen in detail is also quilted in a centre and defined borders layout, but with a signature lotus motif taken directly from the Art Deco style of the building.

Star pattern quilt, 209 x 225cm (82 x 89in), in Turkey Red and white cotton from the early 20th century

Triple X Quilt, *226 x 241cm (89 x 95in), in yellow and white cotton sateen, c. 1910*

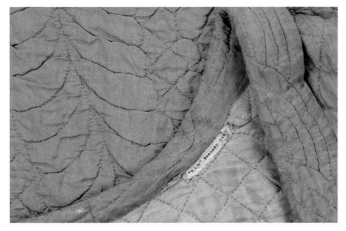

Detail of the blue silk dressing gown made in the Northern Industries Workroom, Barnard Castle in the early 1930s, showing the embroidered nametape

Whilst the Rural Industries Bureau scheme generated orders for quilts to be made in quilters' homes or at classes, the Northern Industries Workrooms established two places of work in Barnard Castle and Langley Moor near Durham in the early 1930s, where employees could complete orders for quilts and other items. Girls and young women learned to quilt at the workrooms and then made quilts, dressing gowns, cushions (pillows) and tea cosies in silks and satin. A blue silk dressing gown with a soft wool filling, now very fragile because of constant use since it was made, still bears the embroidered nametape showing its origin in one of the workrooms.[16]

The Quakers were also involved with helping to relieve the hardship of people living in the mining valleys of South Wales. Through the initiative of Emma Noble, a Quaker from Swindon, Wiltshire, a centre was opened in the Rhondda Valley, South Wales, offering cultural, leisure and adult educational programmes. Sewing and quilting were important parts of the lives of women who attended the centre and, although most of the quilts were made for personal use, some were sent to London for sale.[17]

Between World War I and II, quilting was still used as a means of fundraising. Church Guilds in Hawick in the Scottish Borders worked all year round on quilts, which were then sold for church funds in an annual two-day sale in the town hall. Although close to the quilting communities of Northumberland and Durham, with their distinctive layout style and preferred motifs, the quilters developed their own designs, creating a distinctive 'Hawick' look. The blue cotton sateen quilt (shown opposite), one of 30 quilts made by Janet Pow in the late 1920s and 1930s, contains four hearts in the centre with a border of hearts on the quilt edge. The remainder of the quilt is infilled with Clamshell and not the more typical Square Diamond infill. The hearts are typically Hawick style, with spiky leaf centres. Other motifs favoured by Hawick quilters include thistles and scalloped borders.

Detail of machine-made Comfy quilt showing the commercial label

A great threat to the handmade quilt was the machine-made Comfy quilt. Instantly recognizable by its small size, regular zigzag machine quilting and bordered layout, often with a diamond centre, the Comfy was produced extensively, judging by the numbers that survive. It was made to be reversible with both sides containing a centre and borders of alternating plain and patterned cottons. Sadly, no records of the company making the Comfy have ever been found, but it was one of a number of factory-made quilted bedcovers that contributed to the decline of the individually designed and worked quilt.

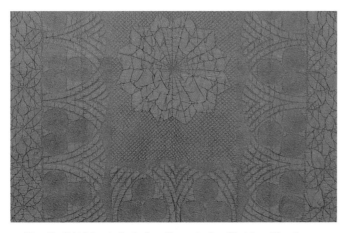

Detail of Welsh wholecloth quilt made for Claridges Hotel, showing a lotus flower motif on the borders

left Wholecloth quilt, *193 x 213cm (76 x 84in)*, made in cotton sateen by Mrs Janet Pow of Hawick, Scottish Borders, in the late 1920s or early 1930s, with detail of central heart motifs *above*

Welsh cotton wholecloth quilt, *196 x 226cm (77 x 89in)*, made for Claridges Hotel under the Rural Industries Bureau scheme in the early 1930s

In the Hour of Need

Any study of British quilt history is not complete without a group of quilts that were not even made in Britain. During World War II, volunteers in a number of allied countries made efforts to help the British cause, and many contributions of aid such as clothing, bandages and bedding were shipped to Britain. The Canadian Red Cross was a leading contributor to the war effort, supplying many items made strictly to standardized patterns and samples in sewing rooms across the country. Quilts were an exception

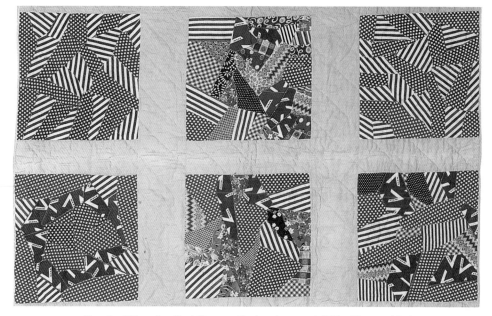

Detail of Canadian Red Cross quilt showing special V for Victory fabric

to the standardization, as noted in a report by the Canadian National Women's Work Committee chairman, Mrs C McEachren: 'One outstanding exception where no samples were required should be noted, namely the patchwork quilts which were made by hundreds of Canadian women in their own homes. They went overseas by the thousand and proved a boon to the British people, especially when the air raids began.'[18] Edmonton Red Cross workers and country branches made 3,231 quilts in 1942 and Nova Scotia alone sent 24,149 quilts between 1941 and 1945.[19]

The quilts and other supplies were shipped into Britain and distributed through the British Red Cross Society, the Women's Voluntary Service (now the Women's Royal Voluntary Service) and the Salvation Army. The quilts were given to people made homeless through enemy bombing or strategic relocation, and to refugees, hospitals and the armed forces. Surviving recipients of the quilts remember overwhelming feelings of warmth towards the generous quilters from the other side of the Atlantic. Many made homeless by bombing, having lost all possessions, recall being given quilts as a first contribution towards a new life.

The surviving quilts can be recognized by a woven or printed label in red and white reading 'Gift of the Canadian Red Cross Society', which was machine stitched to one corner of the quilt back. Because they were not made to pattern, they

could contain a variety of block patchwork patterns showing the taste of the maker. They were made from dress cottons, wools and the new artificial silks of the period. However, many of the quilts were made from simple unembellished Crazy patchwork set in blocks with sashing, as seen in the quilt above, which features two special fabrics with a red or a blue background printed with large white Vs (for Victory) and the Morse code for V: dot-dot-dot-dash. However, many of these quilts were made from more utilitarian fabrics such as striped pyjama fabric or cotton feed/flour sacks.

The quilt made from five vertical bands of randomly pieced strips of a mixture of fabrics, shown right, unusually indicates where the quilters were based. Embroidered in the middle of the central strip is 'Hallville Ont(ario) R(ed) Cross'.

Detail of the Canadian Red Cross Society label

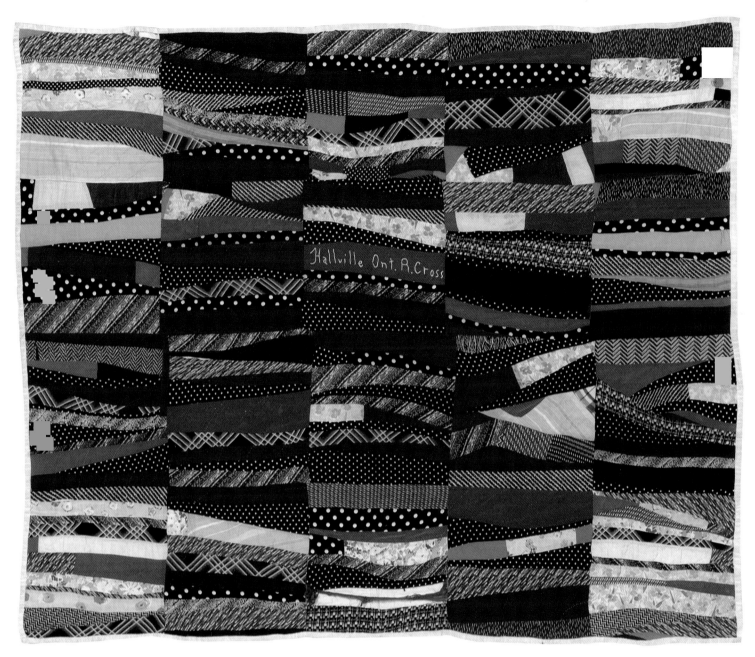

above Canadian Red Cross quilt, *185 x 152cm (73 x 60in),* from Hallville, Ontario

Another Canadian organization called the Imperial Order of the Daughters of the Empire also contributed to the war effort. Founded in 1900 by Mrs Clark Murray to encourage patriotism and social service, the order was open to all Canadian women with a British connection. Chapters of the order united in a common cause and sent clothing parcels mostly comprising of knitted garments and socks to Britain during both world wars. A quilt has been recorded bearing the label 'I.O.D.E.', but it is unknown how extensively members made quilts.

Wholecloth quilt, *220 x 262cm (87 x 103in)*, made by Amy Emms
in 1993 from acetate satin with polyester wadding

Keeping the Flame Alive

After World War II, patchwork and quilting fell out of favour. They were associated with recycling, thrift and making-do, all deeply unfashionable concepts in an era when people were trying to forget rationing and hardship. Women preferred candlewick bedcovers and eiderdowns. A few determined women quilters continued, especially in South Wales and the north east of England, and the skills were passed on at quilt groups formed by the Rural Industries Bureau and at classes.

Amy Emms was one of these exceptional women. Born in 1904 in County Durham, Amy grew up steeped in the tradition of quilting, working alongside her mother to make quilts for a quilt club and for shops in the local town. She continued to quilt after the war, teaching quilting to others so that it 'never became a dying craft' and was awarded an MBE (Member of the Order of the British Empire) for her outstanding contribution to the craft of quilting. She personally took on responsibility for maintaining the traditions of north-country quilting and was often seen at exhibitions and quilt shows demonstrating her skills up to her death in 1998. Her 1993 quilt (left), commissioned by The Quilters' Guild, is a typical example of the fine design and stitch work for which she was known.

Jessie Edwards, another quilting legend, was the teacher of the Porth, Rhondda group, set up by the Rural Industries Bureau in South Wales before World War II. She took part in a quilt exhibition held at the Welsh Folk Museum in 1951,

Detail of cotton quilt with wool wadding
made by Jessie Edwards in 1959

in an attempt to revive interest in quilting, and continued to teach and make quilts to order. A detail of one of her quilts made in 1959 (above) shows the complex nature of her quilt designs and the closely worked quilting stitches.

The influential British quilt historian and quiltmaker, Averil Colby published three books on patchwork and quilting in the mid-20th century at a time when the crafts were disregarded. She had a clear influence over British patchwork of the period, developing a style incorporating many floral fabrics in hexagons and diamonds, which were pieced over papers to make complex flower bouquets, swags and wreaths. Her style was copied particularly through the National Women's Institute where she was chairman of the Handicrafts committee from 1956–61, resulting in a very 'English' look to patchwork at this time.[20] After her death in 1983, her remarkable fabric collection, dating from the end of the 18th to the 20th century, was given to The Quilters' Guild. It now forms the basis of the Averil Colby Fabric Collection.

Pincushions and samples made by Averil Colby
with fabric from her collection

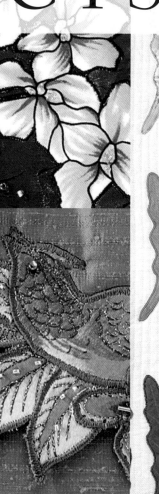

THE PROJECTS

Frame Coverlet, *249 x 283cm (98 x 111in),* believed to have been made by Esther Cooper Cockram Perry in the 1830s

The floral frame coverlet (opposite) is believed to have been made in the 1830s by Esther Cooper Cockram Perry, but it could possibly have been made by her aunt, who was also called Esther Cooper. Esther was married to Reverend Perry of Seighford, near Stafford. A large piece, this coverlet is made from four distinctive highly glazed furnishing cottons, three of which are large-scale, flowing, flower designs, each with a different coloured background of white, blue or dark brown black. The fourth fabric is a large-scale floral stripe on a blue background. Eight large half-square triangles make up the central square, which is surrounded by three pieced borders made from squares on point and triangles, and two borders of fabric with no piecing.

FRAME QUILT
ANNETTE MORGAN

Annette Morgan has created this striking modern frame quilt Framed Taos (right) in response to the Esther Cooper coverlet (opposite). Using techniques such as collage and brainstorming to develop ideas, she has translated the coverlet's key motifs of zigzags, triangles and squares using modern methods of machine appliqué, machine quilting, fabric painting and microwave dyeing.

'I'm no good at drawing – give me a piece of paper and some scissors and I am fine.'

ANNETTE MORGAN

Annette was originally drawn to quiltmaking, not for the design potential of the craft, but 'because it covered a variety of techniques that a competent needlewoman could specialize in'. Though she trained as a nurse, Annette has made her career in quiltmaking, becoming one of Britain's leading teachers and award-winning quilt makers. Ideas are more abundant than time, so Annette uses the quick methods of machine quilting and appliqué, together with foundation piecing. (Foundation piecing is a quick but highly accurate method of sewing fabric pieces together, generally by machine, by following sewing lines marked on a foundation base of cloth or paper.) She also enjoys hand quilting when she has more time.

Internationally known quilters such as Ruth B McDowell, Caryl Bryer-Fallert, Jo Budd and Jane Sassaman provide inspiration, but Annette has established her own distinct style, drawing on her interest in social issues such as the Indian suttee tradition and seeking stimulation from landscapes or ethnic and tribal artefacts.

Frame Quilts

The frame style has been popular in British quilting for three centuries. British quilters created frame quilts using a special fabric, printed panel or strong pieced or appliqué motif for the centre, surrounded by pieced and plain borders. The British Quilt Heritage Project, documenting privately owned quilts (run by The Quilters' Guild 1991–93), revealed that about 15 per cent of the recorded pieced quilts were of the frame style, showing its popularity over time.[1]

Frame quilts can be as simple or as complicated as quilters choose to make them, but if the frames are pieced, a good grasp of arithmetic and drafting skills are needed to fit the patchwork motifs accurately within the frames' dimensions. Many of the surviving frame quilts have striking designs, but the patchwork motifs in the frames are incomplete, suggesting that the maker, although a skilled needlewoman, was not able to calculate the required size of the repeated patchwork shape. Perhaps one of the attractions of the frame style was that quilters could sew patchwork strips independently and only later bring the frames together to make the whole quilt.

Complex frame quilts had many borders, each with elaborate pieced patterns. This is typified by a coverlet from c.1795–1805 (left), believed to have been made in Yorkshire, that features 15 frames fitted into its comparatively small size of 215cm (84in) square. Such a coverlet, entirely hand pieced over paper templates, can only have been made by someone with good sewing and drafting skills, and large amounts of leisure time. Later in the 19th century, much simpler utilitarian frame quilts were pieced by machine or hand running stitch, as the makers came from a level of society where time was not so freely available for quiltmaking.

Complex frame coverlet, 215 x 215cm (84 x 84in), probably made in Yorkshire c.1795–1805

INSPIRATION, RESEARCH AND BRAINSTORMING

Annette is finding new connections between her work and the traditional frame design. She says, 'I like working with the freedom of appliqué and so when I was approached to make a frame quilt [for this project] I was a little surprised. I had made a few pieces that had borders and frames, but I had not considered that these related to the old style of frame quilts. However, the more I pursued the idea of frame quilts, the more I saw that it related to my own work.'

After a trip to Santa Fe, USA, Annette made a series of quilts called Taos Trail. They all featured a zigzag motif drawn from scrapbook and brainstorming exercises, inspired by the frequent lightning storms over the Sangre de Cristo mountains, as well as motifs she saw in Native American jewellery and costume.

When studying British frame quilts, she had also noticed a zigzag pattern often occurring in the frame borders, as we can see in the Esther Cooper coverlet. So she decided to follow the ideas through from the Taos Trail series to create a new design inspired by the frame style.

Annette designs intuitively; after preparatory research, the ideas are allowed to grow through the design process. When a quilt design is drawn from specific source material, Annette collects as many images as possible to give a feel for the subject. These include her own photographs and sketches, together with materials in books, magazines, guides and brochures. Once immersed in a scrapbook of images, she feels ready to brainstorm the colours, shapes, textures and patterns that have become the defining features of the topic. The brainstorming process can help a designer confirm impressions gained during the 'immersion' stage. At its simplest, brainstorming can be time put aside to write down words that freely come to mind when considering the subject. For Annette, the results of a brainstorming session may be a large piece of paper with the topic word at the centre surrounded by defining words, colour patches and sketches of shapes, which are in turn circled by other words taking the description of the topic further (right).

Taos Trail 11 by Annette Morgan, 96 x 96cm (48 x 38in), created in response to her experiences in Santa Fe

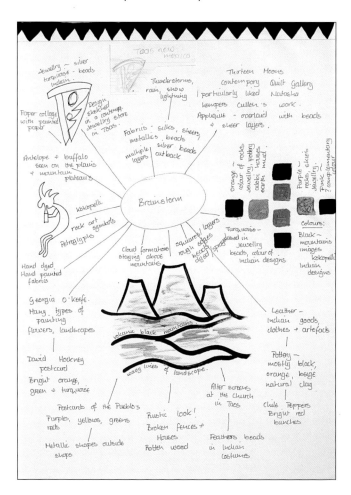

Annette's brainstorm sheet from the Santa Fe trip

Coloured textured papers from which Annette begins her creative process

Collage impression of the Esther Cooper coverlet, using coloured textured papers

Collage from the Esther Cooper coverlet study, also drawing on the Santa Fe study

For this project, Annette looked at as many pictures as she could find of old frame quilts and came up with a list of their features. These included: lots of borders, squares, half-square triangles, medallion centre, zigzag patterns and flowery fabric. She then compared this list with specific features in the Esther Cooper coverlet: the centre square, the triangles set to form a zigzag border, the stripes on the outer border and the colours black, blue, red and green.

DESIGNING WITH TEXTURED PAPER COLLAGE

After the brainstorming, Annette made a textured paper collage (middle left) to give a loose impression of the Esther Cooper coverlet. Such 'paper and scissors collages' are useful to reproduce the impressions created by the brainstorming and then to develop designs from those impressions. Coloured, textured papers can be made easily by marking patterns on coloured paper using brushes, rollers, sponges or blocks, with a variety of paints.

The collages are made by cutting or even tearing the papers to produce shapes, which can be built up to reflect the topic. These could be a free interpretation of a specific image or key shapes arising from the brainstorming.

At this stage Annette was able to pinpoint certain shapes or colour combinations in the collages that she liked enough to develop further – experimenting with changes of scale, spacing, orientation and placement.

Then, drawing on the design work inspired by her Santa Fe trip and the Taos Trail series as well as the Esther Cooper coverlet, she tried more collages before she found a design that she felt had movement, colour and excitement.

She tried other colour schemes such as red, orange, yellow and black which were more related to the Santa Fe ideas (bottom left), but the final design is based on the black, blue, red and green colours of the Esther Cooper coverlet.

During this process of immersion, brainstorming and collage-making, intuition is key for designers like Annette, who is looking for pleasing design elements that she wants to take further. The benefit of such a process is that there is always plenty of unused material to return to when looking for more ideas.

COLLAGE TO CLOTH

Framed Taos went straight from collage to cloth with only some tinkering around to improve the spacing between the motifs and to scale up the collage to a wall hanging. The final collage seemed cramped, so Annette moved the shapes further apart. The collage's colour scheme was retained and Annette decided to reproduce the look of some of the textured papers by painting cotton fabric with acrylic paints. These she applied both by roller and by sponging paint on to the cotton through a thin piece of metal mesh. Acrylic paints do tend to stiffen the fabric, but she considered that this was acceptable in a piece of work intended as a wall hanging.

Annette likes the effect she can achieve by hand dyeing and painting her own fabrics – in this project only the black fabric was commercially produced. She prefers the uneven finish of hand-dyed fabrics to the defined printed images and regular repeat patterns of commercial fabrics. The yellow background fabric was dyed using Dylon cold-water dye before being roller painted with green acrylic. The turquoise-blue and red fabrics were microwave-dyed using Omega Dyrect dyes for cellulose fibres. The turquoise was then sponged with a darker blue acrylic paint.

above Textured papers
below Matching painted fabrics

MICROWAVE DYEING

The bucket dyeing methods often used by quilters for dyeing (for example, with fibre reactive cold-water dyes) need substantial amounts of space and can be messy. Annette is a great fan of microwave dyeing because she can dye quite small amounts of fabric very quickly in each microwave session, as follows.

YOU WILL NEED
Large strong plastic bag
(freezer bags are ideal)

5ml (1 tsp) salt

3–5ml (½–1 tsp) Omega Dyrect
dye powder (amount depends on
strength of colour required)

30ml (1 fl oz) cold water
to dissolve dye

0.25m (¼ yd) fabric to be dyed
(pre-soaked in water until all
the fibres in the fabric appear
to have taken up the water and
then squeezed gently to get rid
of excess water)

Fixing agent such as Synthrapol
or similar

METHOD
1. Put the salt, dye and cold water into the plastic bag.
2. Add the pre-soaked cotton fabric.
3. Squeeze the bag to distribute the dye powders into the fabric fibres. If required, add a little more water to help distribute the dye through the fabric.
4. Place the unsealed bag, opening upwards, in a dish or a strong ice cream container.
5. Microwave on high power for approximately five minutes.
6. Wash and rinse the fabric in soapy water until the water is clear of colour. If the colour bleeds, use a commercial fixing agent such as Synthrapol in the final rinse.

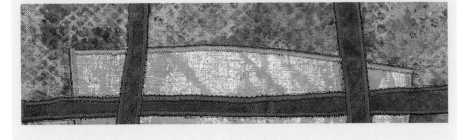

Rectangular reworking of the final quilt design in collage, showing how the ideas can be taken further

CONSTRUCTION

The final design of Framed Taos still features some of the pieced motifs of the Esther Cooper coverlet, such as the zigzag triangles and the squares, but these float freely on a black background. This made it possible to use the easy machine appliqué technique to construct the quilt. The motifs, taken from the final collage, were bonded to the black background fabric using a fusible web (such as Bondaweb), which is ironed to the back of the motifs and to the quilt top. The edges of the motifs were machined using blanket stitch to neaten the raw edges. The whole piece was machine quilted very simply with outline quilting around the motifs and an infill of unevenly spaced straight lines on the black background. Annette chose to make the edges of the quilt uneven since she felt that this was more in keeping with her design. Her final comment: 'I have to say that I became quite excited by the new work and can't wait until I have more time to move the designs on further.'

Chintz

Detail of the Esther Cooper coverlet showing chintz fabric

During the 18th and early part of the 19th century, the term 'chintz' described both dress and furnishing fabrics printed with the full range of colours that could be achieved at that time, using a variety of mordants with red, yellow and blue dyes. The word 'chintz' is actually derived from the Indian word 'chint', for spotted cloth, and relates back to the cottons that were imported from India throughout the previous two centuries.

At this time, both dress and furnishing fabrics were glazed by the calendering process (passing the cloth between heavy rollers, which smoothes and glazes the cloth by applying pressure to the fabric); a very practical process designed to repel dirt. Calendering was abandoned for dress fabric by the second quarter of the 19th century, but furnishing fabrics remained very shiny, as typified by the cottons in the Esther Cooper coverlet.

Chintz gradually came to describe large floral, highly glazed furnishing cottons, often with white backgrounds (the Esther Cooper coverlet's descriptive term in The Quilters' Guild Collection is 'Chintz Frame Coverlet'). The term 'chintzy' then referred to a flowery style of interior decoration and, by the 20th century, was used in a derogatory way – a far cry from the original meaning describing highly sought-after Indian cottons or complex block-printed fabrics.

Framed Taos by Annette Morgan, *96 x 96cm (38 x 38in)*

Red and White Basket Quilt, 202 x 244cm (79½ x 96in), late 19th or early 20th century

The striking Red and White Basket Quilt (opposite) gives us some clues about its origins. The quilting design was marked in blue pencil, the method traditionally used by north-country quilt markers or 'stampers' (see page 77). Combined with the style of the patchwork and the quilting patterns, this suggests that the quilt was made by a skilled quilter from the north east of England at the end of the 19th or beginning of the 20th century.[1] Measuring 202 x 244cm (79½ x 96in), the quilt is made in red and white cotton with alternating machine-pieced blocks of baskets and plain squares. The central blocks are surrounded by a wide, plain border with a basket block in each corner and the entire quilt is heavily hand quilted.

RED AND WHITE QUILT
JO REDNALL

The way the red baskets stood out on the Red and White Basket Quilt (opposite) inspired Jo Rednall to design Stepping Out (right) using the same highly contrasting colours. Her fascination for strong shapes and the potential of using counterchange and the Fibonacci series led to a bold, balanced design in stripes of varying widths.

JO REDNALL

Jo started making quilts at evening class after seeing (and being intrigued by) a Log Cabin quilt at a church fair. Once retired from a career in computing, she spent four years working on the City and Guilds Patchwork and Quilting course. She acknowledges the help received from well-known quilter teachers. 'Deirdre Amsden taught me to hand quilt, use a thimble and use a spoon (!) to help in tacking (basting) the quilt sandwich together.' (Deirdre recommends using a spoon in the free hand to hold the quilt sandwich down immediately in front of where the next tacking (basting) stitch will be sewn – it stops the sandwich lifting up as the needle goes down and up through the layers.) 'Harriet Hargrave made me sit correctly at the sewing machine and opened my eyes a little further to the power of machine quilting.' (Harriet stresses that quilters should look down on their work when sewing, but many use too low a chair, which prevents this.)

When Jo first started making quilts she was drawn to traditional patterns, constantly recreating or absorbing the old patterns and trying to use them in some form. 'I was attracted to the idea of developing a contemporary red and white quilt.'

'On quilts, I found that the Fibonacci stripe structure could be used in various, more complex ways.'

FIBONACCI – A DESIGN INFLUENCE

Jo became interested in the Fibonacci series of numbers whilst at college, where she used the series for ideas on the lines and forms of her designs. The series can be used to create a striped pattern with the widths of the stripes dictated by the numbers in the series. 'On quilts, I found that the Fibonacci stripe structure could be used in various, more complex ways. I could create stripes of widths that increased and decreased as I moved up and down the numerical series. And I could create numerous variations by cutting, rotating and re-joining the striped pieces.'

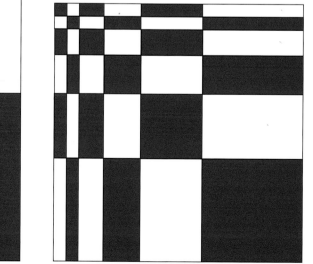

far left Diagram of the Fibonacci series represented as stripes

left Jo's design exercise using the Fibonacci series

Red and White Quilts

Detail of the Red and White Basket Quilt

The combination of red and white is frequently seen in quilts from the second half of the 19th and the early 20th century (see Sawtooth Strippy Quilt, page 98). At this time, many quilts were made by women who could not afford special fabric. They would recycle fabric and make use of fabric samples or factory 'fents' (a general term for ends of rolls, trial runs, misprints or damaged cloth). Often they were limited to the fabrics produced in large quantities for domestic and household purposes. Red and white quilts were made from white cotton generally with a plain (tabby) weave and red cotton called Turkey Red generally with a twill (diagonal) weave. A plain weave is worked when the weft thread goes over and under the warp thread in a regular pattern. A twill weave has the appearance of diagonal lines because the weft thread is worked over one and under two or more warp threads. White cotton was used extensively for bed linen and clothing, and late 19th-century drapers' catalogues show that Turkey Red cotton was sold widely in up to 12 fabric grades for making items such as children's clothing, underwear – and even the first bathing dresses.[2]

Striking quilt designs were achieved with the use of simple pieced or appliqué motifs (generally red motifs on a white background and only very rarely the reverse) and areas of plain cloth in the background were enhanced with detailed quilting. The basket motif was a block design typical of British quilts of the period and one that works particularly well where the colour contrast is high.

Quilters who stitched red and white quilts in the 19th century aimed to make pleasing but functional domestic textiles whilst working to a restricted budget. By the 20th century, when Turkey Red cotton production ended and red cotton became less fashionable for household textiles, the red and white combination became less used. Gradually (probably after the World War I), it came to represent 'blood and bandages', and was thought by some to bring bad luck. Superstitious nurses would not allow red and white flowers to be arranged together in hospital wards. Red and white would certainly not have been the colours of choice for a bedroom or a quilt. Fortunately, as these associations have passed, contemporary quilters are once again exploring the design possibilities of this colour combination.

THE FIBONACCI SERIES

Leonardo Pisano Fibonacci was born in 1170, probably in Pisa, Italy, and was educated in North Africa, where he was taught mathematics. He wrote a number of texts on mathematical topics that were influential in reviving an interest in ancient mathematical skills.

He developed a series of numbers in response to a mathematical problem that was posed concerning the number of rabbits produced in one year by a breeding pair and their offspring living in an enclosed space. Every number in the series is the sum of the two preceding numbers in the series, as follows: 1 1 2 3 5 8 13 21 34 55 89 144 and so on.

A visually pleasing series of stripes or a sequence of geometric shapes such as squares or rectangles can be created by using dimensions dictated by the numbers in the series. This is probably because the numbers in the series are in the same ratio as many proportions of growth found in nature such as the scales on a pine cone or the seeds at the centre of a coneflower (*Rudbeckia*) or sunflower (*Helianthus*).

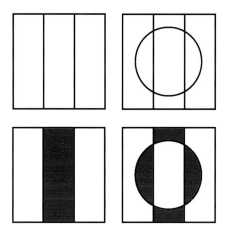

Diagram demonstrating counterchange

Sketch of the final grid of lines with the goose shapes added in the centre

Four painted sketches showing stages of the design development to demonstrate how counterchange alters at each stage

CONTRAST AND SHAPES

In the Red and White Basket Quilt, Jo likes the way the red baskets stand out against the white background. This inspired her to seek out designs that work well with strongly contrasting colours. The alternate red and white triangles in the baskets give the effect of counterchange (a technique where the colours of a motif and its background are reversed in another part of the design). The quilt was 'the catalyst in making me place shapes on [a] Fibonacci series [a stripe design dictated by the Fibonacci series] – I had used both separately, but not together'.

Shapes fascinate Jo and many of her quilt designs evolve from paper cutouts, often after folding and cutting paper at random. It is no surprise that the artist Salvador Dali inspires her because many of the images in his paintings are shapes made up of shapes. Jo has used the traditional American appliqué design Noisy Geese[3] for a number of quilt projects. 'My plan was to use the Fibonacci series to create a red and white striped pattern on to which I would superimpose the Noisy Geese block. The addition of counterchange increased the complexity, creating a positive/negative effect by changing the positions of the red and white colours. The greater the number of components in the design, the more enhanced would be the effects of counterchange.'

MAKING THE DESIGN

Jo decided to make a quilt of just less than one metre (39in) square. 'I drew the design in stages on paper, working to the actual size, beginning with seven vertical stripes of variable width related to the Fibonacci series: 5, 3, 5, 8, 5, 3, 5. The stripe dimensions did not have to fit the Fibonacci numbers exactly, a little leeway does not harm the design.'

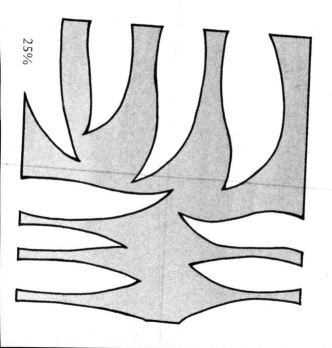

25%

The Noisy Geese block design was scaled up to a size suitable for the dimensions of the quilt and placed on the stripes. Jo scaled up the geese until she was happy with the space they occupied in the centre of the striped background. An easy way of scaling up a picture is to use the enlarging facility on a photocopier. You can create a number of different sizes and experiment with them until you find one that fits the space well. The geese appeared to be walking uphill, so Jo added a path for them to walk on – a horizontal line sloping upwards. 'At this point I felt that the grid [made up of the six vertical lines and one horizontal] was taking on a life of its own and appeared to resemble woods: the vertical stripes had become tree trunks. I added two further lines slanting down from the top of the quilt to represent a shaft of light and to divide up the grid further. Then I included more woodland shapes of leaves, mushrooms and a woodpecker.'

Careful marking of the alternating red and white colours was required to achieve the counterchange effect. Starting at one edge of the top of the vertical stripes and working across the paper, Jo marked a colour change wherever the edge of a shape crossed a vertical stripe.

Noisy Geese Night and Day by Jo Rednall, *35.5 x 66 cm (14 x 26in)*

Turkey Red

The bright Turkey Red cotton was created using a complex method of dyeing involving an alum mordant, which fixes the dye to the fibres of the cloth, and a red dye obtained from the madder plant or its synthesized component, alizarin. The bright colour was achieved by subjecting the cloth to a lengthy treatment with oils or fat before adding the mordant. This 'oiling' allows the mordant to unite well with the cotton fibres, thus producing a good dye result with the madder. The dyed cloth was then brightened in a bath of dissolved tin (stannous chloride). Until this process was discovered only a dull brown red could be obtained when dyeing cotton with madder and alum.[4]

The Turkey Red dye process was introduced into Europe from the Ottoman (Turkish) Empire in the 18th century. It was first used to dye thread, but European refinements of the process led to cloth dyeing. By the first quarter of the 19th century, discharge-printed Turkey Red cotton was produced in a process where areas of the red-dyed cloth were bleached white and colours such as black, blue and yellow were simultaneously overprinted on to the white. The production of Turkey Red cotton expanded through the 19th century, stimulating the growth of specialist dye works in England and Scotland, particularly in the Glasgow area. The cloth was used in Britain and exported extensively, particularly to India, the Far East, West Africa and South America. Interestingly, the Turkey Red cloth produced for the home market tended to be twill weave whilst export cloth was plain weave and often of a thinner quality.

Detail of a late 19th century frame quilt showing discharge-printed Turkey Red cotton

Sample for Geese Dreams showing organza
machine quilted on top of bonded shapes

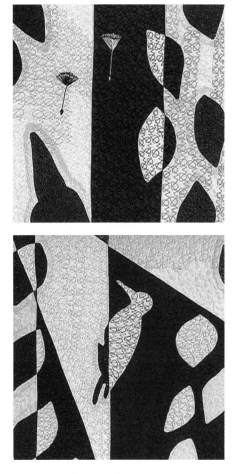

Details of Stepping Out showing *top* hand
embroidered dandelion seed heads and
above machine quilting to give a sense
of dappled shade

CONSTRUCTION

White cotton was used to make the quilt. The red was obtained by dyeing the cloth using a cherry red washing machine dye. The colour subdivisions in some of the smaller shapes required a lot of fiddly piecing even though only two colours were being used, so Jo decided to use reverse appliqué to overcome this problem. In reverse appliqué, two or more fabric layers are assembled. Motifs are created by cutting away the shape required through the top layer to reveal the fabric below and then turning back and sewing down the raw edges of the top layer.

Jo pieced one grid design, without the added shapes of geese and woodland shapes, placing the colours as marked on her paper design. Then she made another grid design to serve as the under layer, with the colours reversed. The two layers were tacked (basted) together; then the shapes were marked on the top layer and stitched using reverse appliqué. The good quality cotton fabric was chosen partly because its tight, fine weave prevents the red areas of the lower layer showing through the white areas of the top layer.

'I machine quilted all over using a variety of coloured and metallic machine embroidery threads to give a sense of dappled shade in the woods. For further embellishment I added dandelion seed heads, hand embroidered in long stitch.'

Jo continued to pursue the red and white colour combination, creating another quilt in the Noisy Geese series – Geese Dreams. 'In this quilt I overcame the fiddly piecing problem, not with reverse appliqué but by bonding the fabric shapes to a base cloth of the stripes. I then laid organza over the whole top and machine quilted the entire quilt surface.'

Stepping Out by Jo Rednall, *84 x 88cm (33 x 35in)*

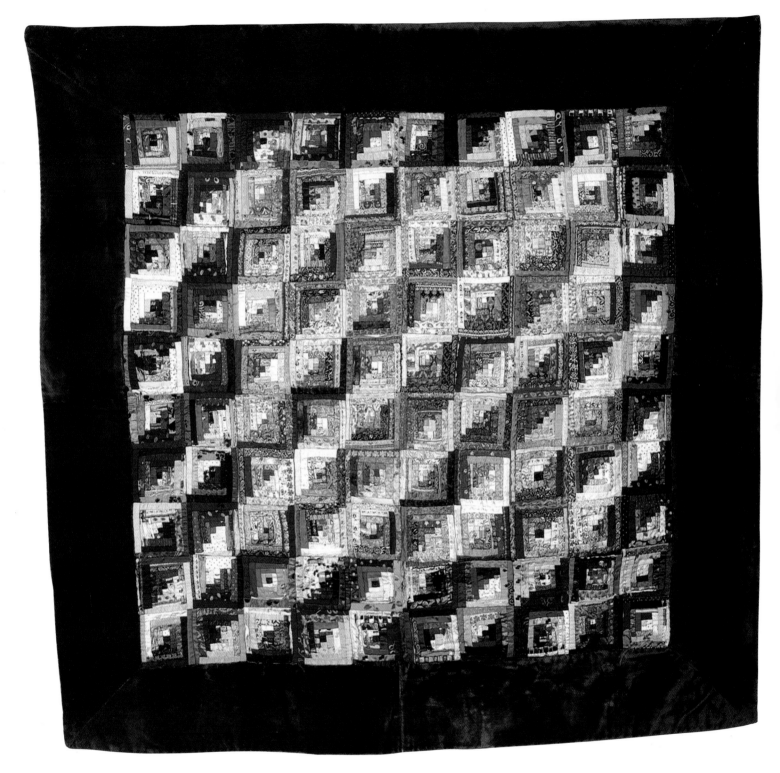

Late 19th-century Silk Log Cabin Table Cover, *122 x 120cm (48 x 47in)*, in silk, velvet and silk ribbon

The rich colours of this small quilt (opposite) draw the eye. Made from silks, velvets and ribbons, the Silk Log Cabin Table Cover was probably intended as a decorative item in a dining or sitting room. It was made towards the end of the 19th century and may have come from Scotland. The Table Cover is made from 100 blocks of Log Cabin patchwork in silk, silk ribbon and velvet in browns, reds, creams and blues, edged by a wide velvet border in rich terracotta brown. The blocks are made by sewing fabric strips around a central square and, in this Log Cabin variation, the darker strips are on two adjacent sides and the lighter strips on the other two sides, giving a diagonal contrast across the blocks.

LOG CABIN QUILT
DINAH TRAVIS

Dinah Travis was inspired by the many different fabrics in the Log Cabin Table Cover (opposite) to use unusual silk prints from her stash for Cross-hatch (right). Departing from the idea of having to make a Log Cabin quilt, she realized that she could still portray that feel with a diagonal furrow pattern. The central strips are left free to fray at the edges.

'My designs are simple in concept … with repeating patterns being an important feature.'

DINAH TRAVIS

The women in Dinah's family were all active needlewomen or craftspeople; there were even Welsh quilts on the beds. Art school trained, it was natural for her to follow the same textile route and 'sewing was easier than oil painting when my young children were around'. She has been making quilts since 1978, led by her childhood memories of bed quilts and she finds inspiration in the painterly qualities of the quilts of Deirdre Amsden.

Dinah has been a leading quilt teacher for over 20 years for City and Guilds and, with fellow quilt teacher Pat Salt, on her own international correspondence course. Log Cabin patchwork was her first focus, but her interest soon widened. She has made traditional quilts to demonstrate design and techniques, and has published books on sampler, appliqué and miniature quilts.[1,2,3] Her quilts are widely exhibited in national quilt exhibitions.

'My own technique has been developed from the need to express ideas in a practical way. All my quilts look quite fragile but will stand up to the rigours of machine washing. I use the rich features of both silk and cotton fabrics intended for fashion or furnishing. Silk pieces are secured by a stitched grid to a cotton base with the edges left free to fray. My designs are simple in concept, with the play of one colour against another, with repeating patterns being an important feature'.

From Start to Finish by Dinah Travis, 100 x 100cm (39 x 39in)

Log Cabin and its Origins

Log Cabin patchwork has been a popular technique since the second half of the 19th century, but in their book *Making Connections Around the World with Log Cabin*, Janet Rae and Dinah Travis highlight the obscurity of its origins. They show similar patterns used in weaving, embroidery, wrappings, mosaics and other ornamentation, including a Log Cabin embroidery pattern seen on stumpwork boxes of the 17th century, but they are unable to demonstrate a direct link.[4] In the middle of the 19th century pattern and ornamentation were closely influenced by classical design and patterns published in a number of design books such as *Grammar of Ornament* of 1856. Such books were influential in popularizing geometric pattern sourced from history and they could have been responsible for acquainting needlewomen with the design,[5] especially as the oldest surviving Log Cabin quilts date from 1850–60.

The traditional way of making a Log Cabin block is to sew fabric strips on to a foundation cloth, rotating the strips around a central square. The strips are either seamed down to the foundation and then flipped over to cover the seam line or folded before tacking (basting) to the foundation with the raw edges covered by the overlapping strip on the next row. The pattern is highly suitable for a wide variety of fabrics because it relies on the effective use of tonal values rather than exact matching of colours or printed patterns.

The tonal contrast between dark and light strips in Log Cabin patchwork is exploited when the blocks are joined together; the blocks can be repeated with the same orientation across the quilt or rotated to create a variety of different layout patterns. In the Silk Log Cabin Table Cover (see page 46), rotating alternate blocks through 180 degrees creates strong diagonal stripes across the piece. The late 19th-century cotton Log Cabin coverlet (below) has the blocks orientated so that the dark sides are together.

During the 19th century, needlewomen from different social classes exploited the Log Cabin pattern, working it in distinctly different styles. Frugal needlewomen in straitened circumstances made utilitarian quilts by recycling household textiles and resorting to cotton, linen and wool fents and samples in a wide variety of colours and print, as typified by the cotton Log Cabin coverlet below. Towards the end of the 19th century this technique was used with silks, ribbons and velvets for more decorative patchwork and was widely mentioned in needlework books, where it was called variously American Log patchwork, Canadian or Loghouse patchwork, Egyptian or Mummy pattern (referring back to ancient wrapping patterns for Egyptian mummies) and Roof pattern. The name Log Cabin has been connected to Abraham Lincoln's 1864 US presidential campaign, but the pattern itself predates this time.[6]

These more showy Log Cabin pieces were often decorated with additional embroidered embellishment as seen in the detail of the Jubilee Quilt (page 52). This quilt uses an unusual Log Cabin method to create the central petals of the flowers by alternating two colours of strips. This unique design was recorded twice during the British Quilt Heritage Project.

Cotton Log Cabin coverlet, *190 x 221cm (75 x 87in),* late 19th century

Dinah's quilt From Start to Finish (see page 48) was the first in a series of quilts based on mazes and Log Cabin blocks. It was made with silk applied to a cotton foundation, frayed and machine stitched to a backing.

INSPIRED BY FABRIC

Dinah has been working with the Log Cabin pattern for some years and initially she had 'no spark of inspiration except to produce yet another Log Cabin quilt!' She usually starts by scribbling with a pen and squared paper to establish a pattern idea and layout, then moving to painting and free drawing. However, this project was different. 'I turned to the fabric and the colour for an idea. The Silk Log Cabin Table Cover suggested the use of many different fabrics, which suited me, as my collection of fabrics consisted of a wide range of small and large pieces of silk fabrics in both plains and prints. These were collected over the years from various sources, [some] dating back to my mother's heyday of dressmaking in the 1920s, remnants gathered from a silk factory in South East London, a collection of dupion silks and donations from friends and neighbours who just left their scraps on my doorstep because they could not bear to throw them away.'

Dinah does not use fabric that is specifically produced for quilters, preferring more unusual materials or plain cloth that she can dye and mark herself. She started with the colours from the Silk Log Cabin Table Cover, 'sorting through what many quilters would think of as a pile of rubbish (no pile of fat quarters for me)'. She selected light colours with a hint of blue and darker tones in a range of warm browns, instinctively selecting a wide

Fabrics from Dinah's stash

Pages from Dinah's sketchbook: diagonals and colours

Pages from Dinah's sketchbook: experiments with borders

range of colours 'reflecting everyday life'. Having arranged the fabric in the order in which they might be used, Dinah could begin thinking about the quilt.

IMPRESSIONS OF THE TABLE COVER

An early decision was to make the project quilt square, so Dinah made many scribbled drawings of Log Cabin quilts in this shape, always returning to the diagonal furrow-like look created by the way the blocks were assembled. She liked the idea of a wide border and looked at the proportions of different widths. 'It took me some time to realize that I did not have to make a Log Cabin quilt to portray the feel of the Silk Log Cabin Table Cover. The diagonal element of the furrow pattern repeatedly kept coming into mind. I made lots of rough paintings of diagonals in blues and browns. I cut them up and gave them various borders. I liked the way the diagonals were coming out on to the border in some of these designs, but felt that the diagonals were becoming too dominant.' Concerned that this would cause a technical problem when she started to sew, she made a small fabric sample to work out how the quilt would be made – 'a simple and practical step' that is often missed, with the result that a quilt can become too complex.

'The sample allowed me to decide on a size of the quilt and how I would apply and piece the fabrics.' Dinah's quilt would be made up of a central square of freely applied strips chosen from the silk prints in her fabric pile and running diagonally from top left to bottom right. The wide border was to be made up of larger pieces of plain silks continuing the diagonal out to the edge in a more subdued range of colours.

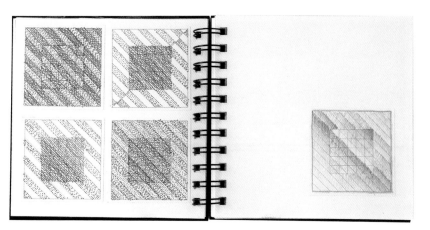

Pages from Dinah's sketchbook: blue and brown diagonals and borders

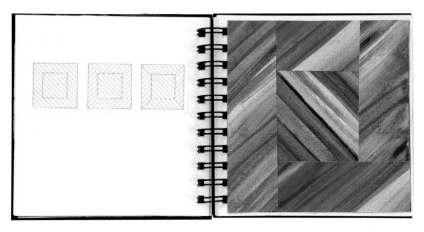

Pages from Dinah's sketchbook: more diagonals and borders

Final design and colouring

Centre detail of Jubilee Quilt (see page 72) made by Mrs Mills in 1887 – the 'flowers' are made by exploiting the tonal contrast seen in Log Cabin patchwork to create bi-coloured petals

MAKING THE QUILT

The strips of the central square were machine sewn on to a cotton square, each overlapping with the edges left free to fray. The border was backed with cotton to balance the weight of the central square and joined to it with a flat seam. The whole quilt was then backed with a cotton square. 'At this stage, I felt that the division between centre and border needed more definition so silk strips were placed round the central square and the edge to act as a narrow border.'

Dinah did more sketches to help make the decision on how to quilt the border. 'To counteract the diagonal, I planned to hand "tack" (baste) quilt the border in columns. The idea of using a large stitch for quilting and a variety of threads came from tacking (basting) together many quilts over the years and being attracted to the way the tacking (basting) stitch was making layers on to one fabric.' She worked diagonally across the quilt following the strips using a wide stitch of roughly uniform length and spacing and various coloured threads, blue tones against the reds and browns and vice versa. The even stitching had the effect of creating raised ridges that ran across the diagonals in the opposite direction.

Dinah considered several ideas for a name for her contemporary quilt around the word 'furrow' such as ploughed, sand ripple, strata, corrugated silk and ribbed. 'Finally Cross-hatch, which means to hatch a surface with crossing sets of parallel lines, was chosen.'

Detail of Cross-hatch

Cross-hatch by Dinah Travis, *91 x 90.5cm (36 x 35½in)*

Bible Coverlet, *115 x 161cm (45 x 63in)*, made some time after 1876

The maker of this small, unusual coverlet (opposite) was possibly from Spennymoor, County Durham, northern England, but her identity is less important than the very specific message she conveys. The Bible Coverlet consists of a number of square and rectangular printed cotton blocks containing scripture quotations, religious music and finely engraved biblical scenes. It was clearly intended to set an example of Christian belief and provide inspiration to anyone who used it. The coverlet was pieced very simply, some time after 1876, with apparently little thought to symmetry or colour balance in the arrangement of the blocks. It was originally loosely backed with a coarse wool fabric, now removed.

QUILT WITH A MESSAGE
HILARY RICHARDSON

The Bible Coverlet (opposite) inspired Hilary Richardson to create Rural Rape (right), her quilt with a message. She developed her ideas by researching dictionary definitions of related words, and collecting photographs, cuttings and printed material. The images were scanned and printed using three different computer-aided techniques.

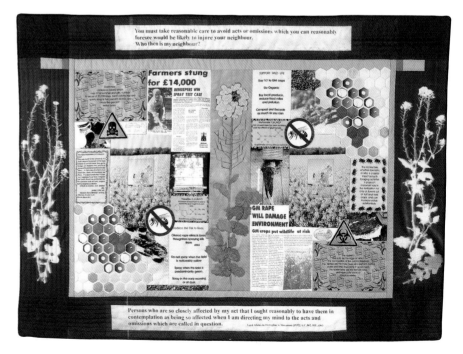

HILARY RICHARDSON

Hilary is both a potter and a quilter. She divides her time between these two contrasting hard and soft crafts, making domestic and commemorative pottery as well as quilts, and teaching patchwork from beginner's level to City and Guilds. She cannot remember a time when she could not sew, knit and crochet; she took up quilting in 1987 because she was drawn to the challenge of its 'precision and geometry'. Hilary tends to use machine quilting techniques because of past medical problems (now cured), but she plans to use more hand sewing methods in the future. Fabric dyeing and printing feature strongly in her work, as do computer-based printing techniques.

Various aspects of her personal life have recently come into Hilary's quilts. Two of them featured feet and shoes because she has unusually small feet. Other ideas revolve around transport and farming issues, and the way people are affected by the activities of nearby farms. She was involved in a court case after she and four other beekeepers lost their bees when a local farmer sprayed an oilseed rape (*Brassica napus*) crop.

'The [Bible Coverlet] design itself is simple, but you cannot ignore the messages.'

Hilary finds a connection with the instigator of the printed scripture blocks, who had 'the courage to have the blocks made because of his own strong beliefs'. Using the techniques already tried in her quilt Shoes (left), she decided to make a quilt to show her feelings about some modern farming practices.

MESSAGES AND ADVERTISING

It is not only religious messages that can be found in patchwork and quilting. Many people have found that simple domestic textiles are a good way of raising funds, supporting a campaign or even promoting a product.

From the end of the 19th century until the 1930s, printed and woven cigarette silks and tobacco flannels were produced as incentives to purchase particular tobacco brands. They were supplied in cigarette packets, wrapped around purchases, or in return for a coupon received with the tobacco. Produced in both Britain and North America, they were aimed at children and needlewomen, even though men consumed most of the tobacco.[1] The manufacturers were able to encourage brand loyalty by tapping into a craze for collecting these silks and promoting the fashion for using them in numerous fancy articles such as cushions (pillows), lingerie cases and tea cosies, such as the one made from printed silks shown far right.[2]

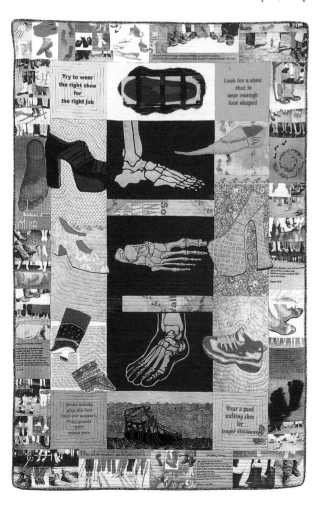

Shoes by Hilary Richardson, 78 x 119cm (31 x 47in)

Printed Scripture Blocks

Only eight quilts and coverlets with printed scripture blocks in the style of those seen in the Bible Coverlet have been identified.[3] The blocks were the work of a Victorian evangelist, Robert Mimpriss, who was inspired to use simple domestic textiles to convey a message of religious conviction to devout families and residents in public institutions such as reformatories, workhouses and hospitals. Although his health was poor, Mimpriss devoted time to designing a series of blocks using suitable religious texts, music and pictures; 126 different blocks have been identified in the eight recorded quilts and coverlets alone.[4] The engraved designs were printed in

Detail of the Bible Coverlet

Crayford, Kent on to cotton fabric of various colours.

After Robert Mimpriss's death in 1876, his widow's agent took over the project and sold the designs in sets of blocks or as made-up quilts. Each block has a number or letter in the seam allowance – a possible guide to the order of joining the blocks and suggesting a very early quilt kit. The sets and quilts were promoted in a temperance magazine called *The British Workman*, but it is unknown how else they were advertised. Three of the coverlets have known Methodist connections and it is documented that chapel sewing groups made up two others.

Many contemporary quilters also use their work to convey feelings and opinions about current issues. Hilary Richardson is one of them. Another such quilter, Michelle Walker says, 'I aim in my work to challenge the association of the word "quilt".' She believes 'it is essential that the content of the work should reflect the time in which it is made'.[5] Her small quilt, House Block, in The Quilters' Guild Nineties Collection was the second quilt she made in response to graffiti about the

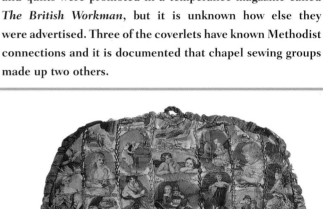

Cigarette silks tea cosy, 1915

House Block by Michelle Walker, 60.5 x 61 cm (24 x 24in)

homeless in Brighton, West Sussex – 'No home, No vote, No job, No chance'. She used plastic material such as bin liners, carrier bags, newspaper and assorted threads and buttons with hand-stencilled lettering.

PREPARING THE MESSAGE

When Hilary begins a quilt on a specific theme, she seeks clues in the dictionary definitions of words connected to the theme. She will often make a list of words and topics that

Collected cuttings and images on the theme

Hilary's photo of work in progress
on the design wall

Image on paper and computer-printed fabric

relate to the theme. She then collects photographs, cuttings and printed material, and finds the Internet useful for researching topics.

For this quilt, Hilary had plenty of cuttings relating to her successful court case, to which she added recent articles on oilseed rape farming, GM rape experiments, beekeepers' reference material and many photographs of bees and oilseed rape plants. This research and preparation stage could be used for a design on any topic. Hilary feels that the time spent collecting the material can also be used to think about how the cuttings and images will work when brought together in a quilt.

Though she may start with a rough idea of how the quilt will look, Hilary expects it to change and develop. She often draws a sketch to show the size and shape of the quilt, and the positions of some of the researched material. However, for her the main design stage is when she starts to arrange her material, adding to it as her quilt design grows. Quilters who design organically often find that using a large area of wall is very useful; the design material can be fixed to it, rearranged and then left for further reassessment. Hilary's design wall is a pinboard covered with a flannelette sheet, but you could hang a sheet down from the top of a wall and pin to that.

ALLOWING THE DESIGN TO GROW

An early decision was to make the quilt rectangular, landscape style, with the centre in a brown frame that has the proportions of a beehive's brood frame (this type of frame is a structure on which the bees build a honeycomb, in this case a honeycomb for the developing young bees). As the layout developed, Hilary transferred the chosen photographs and printed material from paper to cloth, using three different fabric-printing techniques to get the right effect. Two of the techniques were entirely computer based, which restricted the images to A4 (21 x 29.7cm / 8¼ x 11¾in), as that was the largest size of paper her printer would take. This restriction had an effect on the final size of the quilt.

COMPUTER PRINTING ON FABRIC

The first stage was to scan photographs and newspaper cuttings into the computer and print them on to cotton fabric using a computer product called Bubble Jet Set (see page 87 for instructions on computer printing on to fabric).

The printed scripture blocks in the Bible Coverlet were printed generally in black on coloured cotton with a fine engraved border surrounding a central text. Hilary created her own blocks in this style using CorelDraw software. Their content was made up of quotations from her court judgment, descriptions of honeybees and chemical formulae of herbicides and insecticides used on oilseed rape crops, all in a variety of fonts. These were then edged with borders of leaves, flowers and bees. Hilary computer printed these on to coloured cotton that she had dyed with cold-water fibre reactive dyes.

TRANSFER PRINTS

The brightly coloured biohazard chemicals and 'no bees' warning signs, together with the *Chichester Observer* logo, were printed using a transfer printing technique.

To make the honeycomb for the two central corners of the quilt, Hilary hand pieced individual hexagons from white cotton over paper templates. She created transfer prints of hexagons in oranges and yellows, some containing images of the developing bee, and ironed them on to the white hexagons.

Block design and computer-printed fabric

MAKING A TRANSFER PRINT

This method is very effective for images that require a strong colour but will make the fabric stiffer than computer-printed fabric. The images to use for transfer printing are either computer generated or scanned into the computer.

METHOD

1. Use the drawing software to flip the chosen design horizontally so that the design appears to be the wrong way round (later, the transfer process will reverse this back again so that it is the right way round).

2. Check the printer settings options and change to 'T shirt transfers'. Print the flipped block on to computer transfer paper.

3. Check the instructions of the specific product you are using and then iron the transfer on to cotton.

BLUEPRINTS (CYANOTYPES)

Blueprinting is a long-used photographic technique that creates white on blue prints. The white print develops when areas of sensitized paper or cloth are shielded from light whilst the rest of the exposed paper or cloth turns blue. Hilary uses the method to print on to cloth from negatives, which she produces on the computer and also to obtain silhouettes of objects such as plant material by laying them straight on to cloth to make a mask before exposing the cloth to light.

The blueprinted words on the top and bottom borders of the quilt were created using CorelDraw software. The words were typed on to a white filled rectangle

Image, negative and cyanotype

BLUEPRINTING

The cloth requires sensitization in a photographic dark room and the process involves the use of chemicals. Block out all natural light and illuminate the room with a 'safe light' (red covered light bulb). Ensure that the room is ventilated and wear protective clothing, rubber gloves and a face mask. Keep the containers used for the process separate, label the chemicals and the mixed solutions clearly and store them safely.

YOU WILL NEED

- 60g (2oz) ferric ammonium citrate
- 30g (1oz) potassium ferricyanide
- 500ml (16oz or 2 cups) water
- Large shallow tray, such as a cat litter tray
- Perspex or glass large enough to cover both the negative or the chosen object and the cotton fabric
- Rigid board larger than the fabric
- Cotton fabric (washed and ironed)

METHOD

1. Dissolve the ferric ammonium citrate in 250ml (8oz or 1 cup) water. Dissolve the potassium ferricyanide in the rest of the water.
2. In the dark room with the safe light on, mix the two solutions in the shallow tray.
3. Soak the fabric in the mixed solution and hang it to dry in the dark room. Store the remaining solution in brown glass jars for further fabric treatment.
4. Iron the dry fabric in the dark room, place it in two black plastic bags (one bag inside the other) and store it out of the light in a box or drawer.
5. Choose a sunny day for the blueprinting. Put the fabric on the rigid board with a negative or plant material on top and cover with Perspex or glass.
6. Place the covered fabric and board in the sun. The exposure can be from about 5 to 20 minutes depending on the season and the strength of the light, so tests should be done for the right exposure time. If the sun is at a lower angle in the winter, the board should be tilted towards the sun.
7. When the fabric has been exposed, wash it immediately until the rinse water is clear.
8. Dry the fabric. It can then be ironed before use. The print becomes clear and darkens as the fabric dries.

Hilary's photo of blueprinting the rape plant in the sun

and then the 'invert' command was used to turn the words white and the background black. Hilary changed the printer properties/paper setting to 'transparency film' and printed on to computer transparency paper (in this case using three sheets with a little overlap). The three sheets were trimmed and clear taped together to make one long strip of negative, which was used to print on to the fabric. The blueprints on the side borders were created using self-sown rape plants found on the roadside as masks for printing.

THE DESIGN BECOMES THE QUILT

When creating a design, Hilary transfers all the chosen paper designs on to fabric and positions the fabric pieces on her wall until she is satisfied with the design and has an almost finished layout. At this point she makes decisions about how any remaining areas of the design will be treated. In Rural Rape, she wanted the centre section of the quilt to be filled with a rape plant in flower. She cut the plant shape from yellow and green cotton and then bonded it, using a fusible web (such as Bondaweb), on to a blue cotton background that had been transfer printed with an oilseed rape flower head. The brown frame around the centre section has added horizontal lugs (as seen on frames in beehives) with green spacers (the colour chosen to designate the 2004 beekeeping season) running into the border.

The design components were machine pieced, following the layout on the wall. Once the piecing was complete, extra

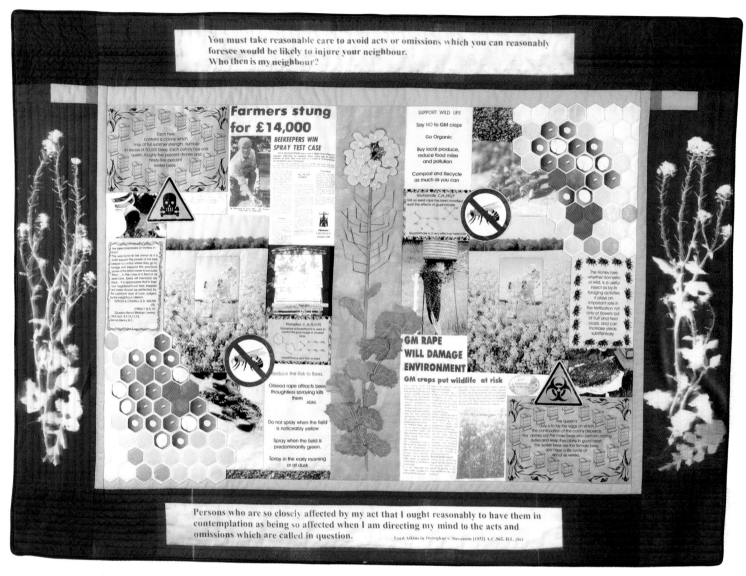

Rural Rape by Hilary Richardson, 92.5 x 128cm (36½ x 50in)

leaves were added to the applied oilseed rape plant, passing across the seams on to adjacent printed blocks. Individual yellow rape flowers were sewn on to the blue background, leaving the edges of the petals free to give a three-dimensional effect. The flowers were embellished with free machine embroidery to create the seed heads and small stalks.

When it came to quilting the piece, Hilary chose to stitch by machine, outlining the blocks and adding rows of lines along the border. The edge was finished with piping. Hilary named her quilt Rural Rape, taking two meanings from the common name for *Brassica napus*.

Happy that her quilt is following the tradition of the Bible Coverlet, she said 'They [Robert Mimpriss and the makers] can have had no idea of the effect these quilts would have, if any, but still did it. The quilt design itself is very simple but you cannot ignore the messages'.

Detail of Rural Rape

Damascus Coat, 19th century

This striking coat (opposite) was probably brought from the Middle East to Britain as a souvenir. Made sometime during the 19th century, it is a typical example of the type of informal coat often made in the Damascus area. Loose overgarments like this would have been worn for relaxed occasions such as gatherings at the bathhouse.[1] The coat shape is simple – square-set sleeves, side slits instead of pockets and no fastenings on the front. Corded quilting creates the interesting surface texture; two layers of fabric are joined by hand-sewn channels down which cotton cords are threaded from the back. The pattern down the front edges and centre back, and along the hem, is made from diagonal and zigzag lines of cording, interspersed with a four-petal floral motif in the body of the coat.

CORD-QUILTED CUSHION
JUDY FAIRLESS

Judy Fairless was fascinated with the play of light on the ridges created by the straight lines of corded quilting on the Damascus Coat (opposite). She could see new possibilities of developing a similar effect in chamois leather. So, experimenting with corrugated paper, she created her Chamois Leather Cushion, a modern design just asking to be touched.

'I am having a "thing" working with chamois (chammy) leather.'

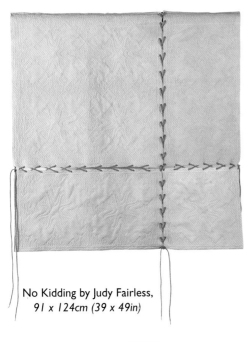

No Kidding by Judy Fairless,
91 x 124cm (39 x 49in)

18th-century baby's cap
using corded quilting on linen

JUDY FAIRLESS

A Quilters' Guild national exhibition in the early 1980s was Judy's first introduction to quilting. Trained as a primary school teacher, she applied her childhood sewing skills first to embroidery, then quilting and she now teaches the City and Guilds Patchwork and Quilting course. Judy has developed a reputation for elegant quilt designs, often with subdued colouring.

Judy likes to mix the two crafts of embroidery and quilting, using many different machine piecing and quilting techniques. Currently, she says, 'I am having a "thing" working with chamois (chammy) leather. My experiments with machine quilting on leather resulted in interesting effects enhanced by the grain of the skin, so I want to develop this technique – the only thing holding me back is the difficulty of getting the leather in large enough pieces.' This is not a new problem. A needlework dictionary for 1882 features kid patchwork, 'this patchwork is generally confined to the making of such small articles as pincushions, slippers or mats, as the kid generally used for the purpose is cut from old gloves, and therefore is not of a large size; but if the pieces can be obtained of sufficient size cushions (pillows), footstools and other large articles may be attempted'.[2] Judy's quilt No Kidding is an updated wholecloth quilt inspired by a study of shoes, worked in chamois leather with the sections joined by long bootlaces.

Judy keeps a number of notebooks on various design themes and is constantly adding to them. She studies a design source, pattern or motif and reproduces it by drawing, printing or paper cutting. Using tried and trusted design methods, she will then play with the motifs by creating pattern repeats, rotating and mirror imaging the design. Her books are filled with pages of patterns reproduced in many ways, from plain lead pencil to vibrant colour – all waiting to provide inspiration for future work.

THE FASCINATION WITH CORDED QUILTING

Corded quilting is very much an 18th-century technique; items of 19th-century work in Britain are rare. In the early 1920s and 1930s there was a revival of interest in the technique amongst amateur embroiderers. Renamed Italian quilting, it was used for decoration on small objects such as cushions (pillows) and sachets, and for the centres of feather-filled eiderdowns, often worked in fine silk or even one of the early synthetic silks.

Contemporary quilters are exploring the potential of the method. Helen Parrott made a series of quilts using corded and stuffed quilting, inspired by the ancient cup-and-ring markings seen on the Yorkshire Moors. Her small quilt, Ilkley Moor 1981 (top right) in The Quilters' Guild Nineties Collection, is part of this series.

Judy is fascinated by corded quilting and especially its ridges. 'For this project, I saw new possibilities in working corded quilting on leather. I studied the traditional motifs seen in 18th-century cord-quilted garments such as the baby's cap (below left), then experimented with the flower and leaf motifs in my sketchbook.' Gathering the patterns together, she sketched some possible uses for the designs on small caps and bags. Using one of the floral designs, she worked a sample of corded quilting in tan brown mock suede, sewing the channels by machine. She decided that the resulting patterns, though attractive, were not sufficiently innovative and the curves were awkward to machine sew.

FROM CURVES TO LINES

Judy was increasingly drawn to the straight-line patterns on the baby's cap (below left) and the Damascus Coat. 'I decided to abandon the curves of the floral designs for the jagged zigzag effects of the lines and went "back to the drawing board" to experiment with more patterns.'

Pieces of corrugated paper were useful in representing the relief effect of lines of corded quilting. Large-scale corrugated paper was stuck down in patterns with squares and triangles of paper to study the play of light and shade across the ridges. The resulting patterns were best suited to a square design, ideal for a small item such as a cushion (pillow).'

Judy experimented with a variation of corded quilting by inserting cords into channels from the top surface, leaving the ends showing. Unwittingly, she was referring back to earlier decorative techniques using cords. In the 18th century, men's

Ilkley Moor 1981 by Helen Parrott, 61 x 61.5cm (24 x 24in)

cord-quilted waistcoats often incorporated pulled-thread or embroidered infillings with surface applied cords in an imitation of lace. A pair of embroidered silk sleeves from the 17th century in the Victoria and Albert Museum, London, has 'S' lengths of satin-covered cotton cord couched down on to the silk surface in a wave pattern grid.[3]

The worked leather samples helped Judy to decide her final design. She created the surface cording by applying a patch of leather on to the top surface and sewing channels across it. This looked best if space was left between the blocks of cording. 'I found that diagonally sewn channels distorted the leather. I liked the contrast of a brown cord (shoelaces) with the cream leather, so I left the ends of the cords as tufts.'

Impressions of floral motifs taken from two babies' caps: in paint, ink and string

Half-floral motif used as border patterns

Corded Quilting in Clothing

Corded quilting gives textural pattern and body to a fabric without the warmth-giving layer of wadded quilting, but it is very labour intensive because making the hand-sewn channels for the cording, and threading the cords neatly from the back, takes a long time. There are many surviving 18th-century examples of bed coverings and clothing made from corded quilting. At this time, quilted garments were an important part of men's and women's wardrobes, and corded quilting was frequently used for men's waistcoats, women's jackets, formal and informal gowns, as well as babies' gowns and caps.[4] There was a flourishing trade in professionally made wadded and cord-quilted clothes, ready-made and to order (the latter with greater variety in design). The waistcoats were often sold as uncut panels, to be made up to fit the purchaser.[5,6] The handwork on cord-quilted garments was expensive, so this

Baby's cap – corded quilting on linen with pulled work and French knots, 18th century

was clothing for the wealthy, but it was also more practical being easier to launder than the fashionable fancy woven silk fabrics.

There was a long-established hand quilting industry based around the area of Marseilles, southern France, so items of corded quilting or *broderie de Marseille* made in white cotton were widely known across Europe during the 17th and 18th centuries.[7] French bedcovers worked entirely in corded quilting were highly sought after, at a price, since they would have taken many hundreds of hours to make. *Broderie de Marseille* was imported into Britain, but there was also a thriving domestic quilting industry. Trade cards from 18th-century businesses in London advertised both wadded and 'French' quilting, the latter term referring to corded quilting. English ladies who could not afford the imported French goods could purchase locally made items as well as the marked cloths and cotton cords to work the corded quilting themselves.[8]

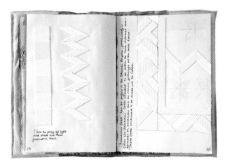

Line patterns from the Damascus Coat using corrugated paper

Designing using corrugated paper

Final design for the cushion (pillow), in paper, corrugated card and wool

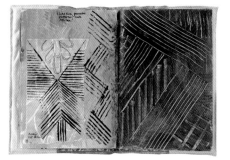

Line patterns

A LEATHER CUSHION

Judy created a mock-up for the final design for the cushion (pillow) using brown and white paper, corrugated card and cream wool. The centre was to be surface cord quilted, with a wide straight edge to the cushion in standard corded quilting, where the cording would be hidden on the back.

With the design transferred to tracing paper, Judy machine stitched the channel design for the border through the paper on to the leather top, which was backed with cotton fabric. She applied square patches of leather for the surface cording and stitched channels for cording with the brown shoelaces. The back of the cushion (pillow) was decorated with a panel of surface cording and a feature was made of the opening by adding metal eyelets and brown cord lacing.

All the sewing was done using a machine needle for leather. 'A walking foot was useful for all the straight sewing and I sewed the surface corded squares using a zipper foot.'

FINAL RESULT

Judy plans to continue her 'thing with chammy leather'. She said: 'I like the tactile feel of the leather. When it is combined with the textural designs of corded quilting, it is just asking to be touched.'

above Chamois Leather Cushion by Judy Fairless, 50 x 50cm (19¾ x 19¾in)

left Back of Chamois Leather Cushion with surface cording, eyelets and lacing

Flower Tea Cosy, *36.5 x 23.5cm (14 x 9in)*, **early 20th century**

This undeniably charming tea cosy (opposite) is only 23.5cm (9in) high, but it is made from many irregular patches of silk and velvet, each heavily embellished with delightful floral and decorative embroidery. Made at the beginning of the 20th century, the Flower Tea Cosy was found in a charity shop and donated to The Quilters' Guild in 1992. It is a fine example of Crazy patchwork, which is usually found on larger covers, throws, cushions (pillows) or coverlets, such as the Irish Crazy Patchwork Coverlet (page 71) made in 1880 by Elizabeth Ferguson.

CRAZY QUILT
LINDA KEMSHALL

The random shapes of the Flower Tea Cosy (opposite) reminded Linda Kemshall of the fragmented nature of mosaics and parched desert landscapes. She hand dyed and painted fabrics to give subtle colour changes, broken by a strong fracture line across her quilt, Fracture (right). A simplified grass shape, worked in hand and machine stitching provides a strong connection to the traditions of Crazy patchwork.

LINDA KEMSHALL

Linda claims that she came to textiles by a circuitous route. Trained as a painter and having sewn from childhood, she was introduced to quiltmaking when she worked with a colleague who made patchwork in her tea break. The hobby soon developed into a full time activity after Linda took the City and Guilds Patchwork and Quilting course, achieving their Medal of Excellence in 1995. Linda has taught City and Guilds courses in the UK and the USA and, since 2001, online. She is now an external verifier and National Advisor for the City and Guilds Patchwork and Quilting course.

Linda loves colouring cloth and is very comfortable with all the fabric painting and dyeing techniques. 'With the wealth of products available now, I can achieve the painted effects on fabric that I have so long loved on paper.' The quilters she admires most, like Michael James, Nancy Crow and Erika Carter, are similarly able to colour, paint and print cloth to stunning effect. Linda's book *Colour Moves – Transfer Paints on Fabric* was published in 2001.[1] Linda is well known for her very painterly quilts, many of the early pieces being figurative, as seen in her quilt Demons in My Head (below) for The Quilters' Guild Nineties Collection. A continuing theme has been feathers, angels and birds; some of her most striking quilts have featured the crows often seen around her south Staffordshire home.

'I can [now] achieve the painted effects on fabric that I have so long loved on paper.'

above Pages from Linda's sketchbook: detail of the Flower Tea Cosy with patterns from the stitches

INSPIRATIONS

Linda's painter's eye is always open for interesting designs, patterns and colours – constantly seeking new images to explore. Working with oil pastel and watercolour, she fills her sketchbooks with landscapes, rock formations and architecture as well as birds and feathers. For this project, she started with images of the Flower Tea Cosy and then added her impressions of the randomly shaped, coloured cloth and the embroidery stitches.

Linda often begins a design by brainstorming words and phrases. 'I was drawn to the fragmented nature of the Crazy patchwork and saw connections both with mosaics (such as those in the buildings designed by Antonio Gaudi in Barcelona) and parched desert landscapes. I studied the "crazy" nature of these two diverse themes, and painted and drew images in my sketchbook. The fragments in the images led me to the idea of fractures, so I experimented by cutting apart segments and rejoining them, often with staples. I also admired the embroidery in the tea cosy, especially the shaded colours of the flowers and leaves, so I added a simplified version of a grass shape to my drawings and this motif became a strong feature in the design.'

Demons in My Head, 60 x 61cm (23½ x 24in), by Linda Kemshall, made for the Nineties Collection in 1997

Crazy Patchwork

Crazy patchwork, very popular during the late 19th and early 20th century, was usually worked in luxury fabrics such as silks and velvets to create decorative items not intended for heavy use. It has been suggested that Crazy patchwork was inspired by the Japanese textiles seen in the exhibitions held in Europe and the USA during the second half of the 19th century, a time when Japanese decorative arts captured the imagination of the western world.[2,3] Crazy patchwork was soon mentioned in needlework books alongside embroidery and in 1882, it was featured as Puzzle patchwork in a British dictionary of needlework.[4]

In Crazy patchwork, randomly shaped fabric pieces are laid on to a foundation cloth, each piece overlapped on one edge by the adjacent piece. Once tacked (basted) to the foundation, the pieces are attached by embroidery stitches along the edges of the pieces, which also neatens them. At its simplest, the embroidery may be herringbone or feather stitch, but heavy embellishment is seen on many items from this period.

Canadian Red Cross quilts, which were brought into the UK in great quantities during World War II (see page 24), were often made using Crazy patchwork. Because these were utilitarian quilts they were not heavily embellished.

Irish Crazy Patchwork Coverlet, 208 x 229cm (82 x 90in), made by Elizabeth Ferguson in 1880 using silks and velvets

PUTTING THE IDEAS INTO THE QUILT

Linda likes Crazy patchwork because it is 'an ideal method for free appliqué designs with a painterly sense of colour'. To bring together elements of Victorian Crazy patchwork with Gaudi's distressed mosaic surfaces and images from deserts, she chose a random shape with washes of colour. 'Crazy patchwork was usually worked with contrasting colours so that the shapes stood out, but I wanted the colour changes to be far subtler so that the shapes gradually become apparent when the quilt is viewed more closely. Starting with pale desert colours at the top of the quilt, the colour would become darker and change downwards to deeper blues, reds, greens and purples drawn from Gaudi's mosaics. I wanted the colour change to be emphasized by a strong fracture running diagonally across the quilt, the two parts connected by beads, which would also be added as final embellishments across the quilt.' (Many of Linda's recent quilts have been made in segments linked with cords or beads.)

Pages from Linda's sketchbook: *above* showing impressions of a parched desert landscape and *below* showing images of fragments and fractures cut and stapled together with added grass seed heads

Embellishment on Quilts

At certain stages in British quilt history there was a fashion for heavy embroidery on patchwork to enhance plain fabrics. The fashion faded when printed fabrics became the popular materials for quiltmaking. Amongst the few surviving items of patchwork from the early 18th century are a coverlet and a coverlet fragment, which are extensively embellished together with added embroidered and appliquéd motifs known as slips.[5] The coverlet and the fragment were pieced from a variety of silks and velvets and,

Silk and velvet Jubilee Quilt, *202 x 204cm (79 x 80in)*, made by Mrs Mills in 1887 to celebrate Queen Victoria's Golden Jubilee

whilst some of the fabrics are fancy decorative weave silks, many are brightly coloured but plain woven. The strong tradition in both professional and domestic embroidery of that time is reflected in these two patchwork pieces.

Later in the 18th century, fashionable printed cottons and linens came to be 'shown-off' in patchwork, so the distraction of added pattern was not desirable. An exception was Broderie Perse coverlets and quilts, where embroidery was often added (see the Tree of Life coverlet on page 106).

Pure patchwork without embroidery continued to be the preferred style into the 19th century. It was only when there was a move back to using silks and velvets later in that century that embellishment again became popular in British patchwork. The luxurious silks, velvets and ribbons used for Crazy, Log Cabin and Mosaic patchwork on showy table covers, throws and coverlets often became a medium for extra decoration. Such ostentatious, heavily embroidered surfaces chimed well with the furnishing style of the richer classes.

The striking complex silk and velvet frame quilt shown here is an example of such decoration. Made by Mrs Mills in 1887 to celebrate Queen Victoria's Golden Jubilee, it was sewn for a family in lieu of rent. The entire quilt is covered in embroidery and the outer border of fans in particular contains flowers, animals and figures including fashionable ladies and children playing with toys.

In the second half of the 19th century, quilters could find embroidery stitches and designs in ladies' magazines and needlework books.[6] The stitches were worked in a variety of threads and, in Crazy patchwork, were often accompanied by buttons, braids, beads and sequins to add extra sparkle.

MAKING FRACTURE

Linda normally makes quilts using cotton and linen, but here she used a wider range of hand-dyed and painted fabrics. The construction of Fracture was straightforward; fabric pieces were placed randomly but with thought given to colour and tone, and sewn down on to a backing. Linda layered much of the quilt with fine gauge net in colours to match the colour changes across the quilt. Some of the net was then cut back to provide extra texture. She used the grass motif across the quilt, stitching it both by hand and machine in mostly self-coloured threads but making it more obvious nearer to the fracture line by using contrasting colours. To give stability and prevent the quilt sagging along the fracture, the top was layered and machine sewn on to a backing.

Linda used three disparate design sources to create her quilt: 'I saw parallels with the fragmented shapes present in all three, the final piece is the coming together of these apparently diverse strands. It was intended as a one-off for this project, but I am inspired to make more work in a similar vein.'

Fracture by Linda Kemshall, 98 x 146cm (38½ x 57½in)

Wholecloth Quilt, *170 x 258cm (67 x 102in)*, with central oval medallion c. 1920s

The simple cream cotton sateen fabric of this wholecloth quilt (opposite) has been transformed into a striking bedcover by the complex design of its hand quilting. Made in a style often described as central medallion and border, it is typical of quilts made in the north east of England in the late 19th and early 20th centuries and was probably made in the 1920s. It carries a small handwritten label 'Mrs Maughan £3.5.0 [£3.25]', which may indicate that it was made to order.

The centre of the quilt contains a defined oval enclosing a complex combination of quilt motifs. The outer border of repeating curved leaf motifs is also illustrated in a paper on the quilt designers of north east England.[1] The quilt has never been used and bears only the marks of being folded for years and blue pencil marking the design.

WHOLECLOTH QUILT
SHEENA NORQUAY

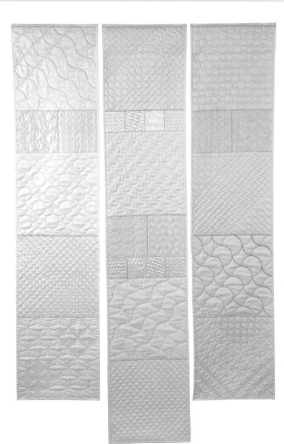

The Wholecloth Quilt (opposite) provided Sheena Norquay with the challenge of designing a sampler of grids suitable for free machine quilting. In designing her three-panel quilt, CGP Panels, she explored the possibilities of traditional infill patterns and chose threads in beiges, greens and blues as a link back to the blue pencil marks on north-country quilts.

'Whenever an idea comes into my head, I scribble ideas and do quick sketches. I love doodling with lines.'

SHEENA NORQUAY

Over the last 20 years, Sheena has made the journey from primary school teacher to freelance quilt teacher and lecturer, with a reputation for striking quilts exhibited widely in national exhibitions. She learned to sew as a child: 'I was drawn to quilting for its sculptural quality and the way it can add movement and texture as well as shapes and motifs to cloth.'

Sheena's two preferred quiltmaking techniques have influenced the style of her quilts. She has produced a series of complex appliqué designs often connected to mythology and her home in the Orkney Islands. Going Home (below right), made for The Quilters' Guild's Nineties Collection, refers to Sheena having to cross the sea to the Islands. 'I sit on the beach as a mermaid with my two cats gazing longingly at the distant land, surrounded by symbols referring to the sea, legends, hope, patience and the passage of time until I can return.' Complex free machine quilting is her other love. She uses it to both enhance appliqué designs and to make striking wholecloth quilts, often laid out sampler style and coupled with subtle changes of colour through softly coloured machine quilting thread, printing and stencilling.

SCRIBBLING, DOODLING AND DRAWING

Sheena's notebook lives with her at all times – beside her bed and when travelling. 'Whenever an idea comes into my head, I scribble ideas and do quick sketches. I love doodling with lines.' For a pictorial piece, 'I usually do research and mull it over for a while before making it. With an experimental piece, I think about options for techniques, fabrics and layout. Again I make lists of ideas to choose from.'

She has been experimenting with grids for some time, including a combination of printed dots, rings and decorative lines within the restriction of a grid or block. She sketches and then accurately draws the patterns, which she will reproduce in her wholecloth quilts, as samplers of simple repeated shapes (see page 79).

Details of the Wholecloth Quilt showing *far right* the border pattern and Square Diamond infill and *near right* the centre detail

Quilt Stampers of the North East of England

From the second half of the 19th century into the mid-20th century, a localized industry of quilt designing flourished in the north east of England. Individuals earned a living by marking quilt designs on quilt tops, generally for wholecloth quilts, but also for strippy and pieced quilts. Blue pencil was used to mark the quilting lines and the similarity of this effect to blue stamped transfer patterns for embroidery might have led to the description, used colloquially, of quilt 'stampers'.[2]

The designers received wholecloth and pieced tops (see Triple X Quilt on page 21) from quilters across the north east or provided their own marked tops for sale. The standard cost for marking was still only 1/6d (7½p) until the 1930s.[3] The designed quilts are distinguished by a complex combination of motifs in the centre of the quilt, a wide flowing border that is broken at the corners by different groups of motifs and Square Diamond infill across the remaining body of the quilt. They stand out against other wholecloth quilts from the area, which also may have been marked in blue, because of the quality of the design and the skilled and confident way the designs, and particularly the infill, were drawn. The designers worked with their own favourite quilt motifs on templates, which they supplemented with extensive freehand drawing of flowers, leaves, stems and scrolls. The quilting motifs had a distinctive regional style and were often based on nature, with formalized flower and leaf designs together with feathers, shells and chain patterns. Two unique designs

have been noted. An oval shape described as a flat iron is usually infilled with a rose, leaf and scroll pattern. The other is a freehand drawn open scroll with an added plumed outline, a variation of which can be seen in the Wholecloth Quilt with central oval medallion (see pages 74 and 76).[4]

The designers were based in two valleys, Weardale and Allendale, in the north Pennine dales of Northumberland and County Durham. The establishment of the quilt designing trade is ascribed to a George Gardiner, a draper in Allenheads, Allendale, who trained local girls to quilt and mark quilts probably from the 1870–80s.[5] One of his apprentices, Elizabeth Sanderson, carried on designing and marking quilts in Allenheads until her death in 1933. She took in her own live-in apprentices from the last decade of the 19th century and although few quilts can be attributed to her hand, her influence over the development of the quilt style cannot be denied. However, a Star frame-pieced design can be attributed to her.[6] Generally white with another colour such as red, blue or pink, this striking design was widely available from quilt designers or bought from travelling salesmen.

Another professional quilt marker was Miss Mary Fairless, who continued to mark quilts until retiring in her 80s in 1989.[7] At the age of 19 she had worked with a Mrs Peart, who had been apprenticed to Elizabeth Sanderson, learning to be a pattern marker, and had then continued alone, maintaining a tradition that has flourished since the last quarter of the 19th century.

GRIDS AND SQUARE DIAMONDS

The infill between the quilt patterns in old wholecloth quilts tends to be overlooked. However, the ubiquitous Square Diamond infill (also called Hanging Diamond) seen in north-country wholecloths is very difficult to draw accurately. Well drawn, it is one of the features that distinguishes quilts marked by a quilt stamper. The style of these quilts allows for large areas of infill, which enhance the complex groupings of patterns around them.

During other periods of British quilting and in other regions, the infill has been treated in different ways. In the Cockburn wholecloth quilt (see page 78), made earlier in the 19th century, lines separate the complex central circle design from the borders, and the infill does not link the different areas together. Other infill patterns such as Clamshell were used and can be seen on the wholecloth quilt from Hawick made by Mrs Janet Pow in the 1920–30s (see page 23).

Going Home by Sheena Norquay, 62 x 63cm (24½ x 25in), commissioned for The Quilters' Guild Nineties Collection

Cockburn wholecloth quilt, 228 x 240cm (90 x 94½in), from the second quarter of the 19th century

Sheena was drawn to the infill in old quilts, 'I wanted to set myself a challenge to design and make a sampler of grids suitable for free machine quilting. I looked at the features of infill patterns in old quilts and listed straight lines (crossing diagonals or horizontal and vertical), curved lines in Clamshell and Wineglass, equal spacing of lines, diagonals crossing at different angles to make squares or diamonds, fabrics often with a sheen and threads matching or slightly darker.' From

the list, Sheena chose a curved line, wanting to see how many pattern variations she could draw whilst still making it easy to sew on the machine.

'I set myself some parameters so my drawings could keep a feel for the features of traditional infill pattern using regular spacing to the grids in three different scales. I wanted to concentrate on variety in pattern design using curved lines.' Sheena drew designs in three different sized blocks – 7.6cm

(3in), 15.2cm (6in) and 30.4cm (12in) – allowing one size of spacing in the smallest block, two in the middle-sized block and three in the largest block. She created diagonal grid patterns for the largest block, horizontal and vertical patterns in the middle-sized block and a mix of both for the smallest block.

She said: 'This was quite absorbing when playing with the pattern possibilities, but a bit monotonous to draw out the small-scale grids on the 30.4cm (12in) block. I decided at that stage to break up some of these patterns on the 30.4cm (12in) block to add a bit of interest by adding, subtracting and changing some of the lines. I also planned to flatten some areas within the grid with heavy stitching when I got to the machining stage. The designing and drawing of the grid took 19 hours.'

25 by Sheena Norquay, *100 x 100cm (39½ x 39½in)*

STITCHED SAMPLES

Sheena chose fabrics that had a subtle sheen – cotton sateen, silk cotton mix, silk and satin. She discarded the silk cotton mix after it shrank when she wet and ironed it. She stitched samples of the grids using the remaining three fabrics, experimenting with different machine needles and threads. 'Satin distorts when machined in larger pieces so I decided to use it for the smallest blocks only. I would use silk dupion for the 15.2cm (6in) block and sateen for the largest blocks.'

The original plan was to make a frame-style sampler with a square of 7.6cm (3in) blocks in the centre surrounded by borders of the other two sizes of block. 'Because of the distortion problem, I decided to change to three panels made up of the three sizes of blocks.'

MACHINE QUILTING

Free machine quilting is done by dropping the feed dogs in the sewing machine, setting the stitch length to '0' and using a darning or quilting foot. 'I do all my quilting using a 25.5cm

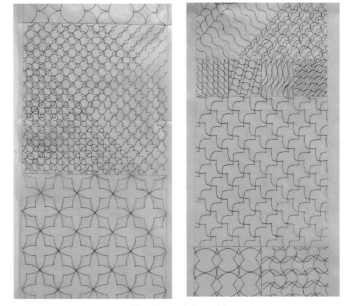

Drawings of the grids

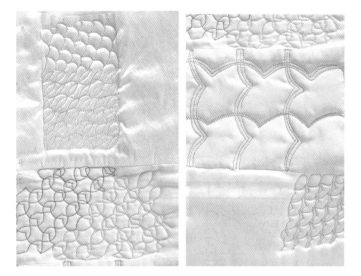

Stitched samples: experiments with fabric and thread

MARKING AND MACHINING

Successful quilting can only be achieved after careful marking of the design on the fabric. Sheena did not want the marks to be obvious, so she traced the design using a propelling pencil, resorting to a light box for the more intricate patterns. She chose a number of pale pastel shades for the threads, including beiges, greens and blues; the subtle colouring of the stitching was a link back to the blue pencil marks of north-country quilts. 'On some of the larger grids, I flattened different areas of the background with heavy stitching to add interest to the block and show the various ways it could be quilted. I quilted the grids from top to bottom on each panel, working the grid lines in straight and satin stitch and then separating the blocks with satin stitch.

Quilting the grids took about 13 hours. The extra quilting, trimming thread ends and binding the panels took me another 24 hours.'

NAMING THE PANELS

'Before I finished quilting the panels, I had to have my last remaining cat put down, so many tears were shed during the final quilting and completion of the panels. It occurred to me at this time to call the panels the CGP Panels in memory of my cats, who have brought me so much pleasure over the last 11 years. I have quilted a cat together with its name on each panel – Cuddles, Garfield and Persistence. This was the last piece of work 'supervised' by Cuddles. You may still find one of her hairs somewhere on the panels.'

(10in) hoop, but you can use just your hands to hold the quilt layers.' Attaching the three layers of the quilt 'sandwich' together firmly is important. 'I tacked (basted) the panels in vertical and horizontal lines approximately 5cm (2in) apart.' Other quilters prefer to pin the layers together.

It is important to try samples of fabric, wadding (batting), thread and needles before starting so that materials can be rejected if unsuitable, as Sheena discovered with the silk and cotton mix fabric. Wadding (batting) can be a significant influence over the final result and a firm, but thinner thickness is best. For this project, Sheena chose Hobbs wool wadding (batting). She was prepared to cope with frequent changes of needles and thread in order to achieve the best effect. 'I used Madeira cotton tanne no. 50 with a machine quilting needle, Mettler no. 100 with a size 10 jeans needle and Sulky metallic thread with a metallica or heavy metal needle.

Detail of CGP Panels, showing machine-quilted grids and Sheena's cat

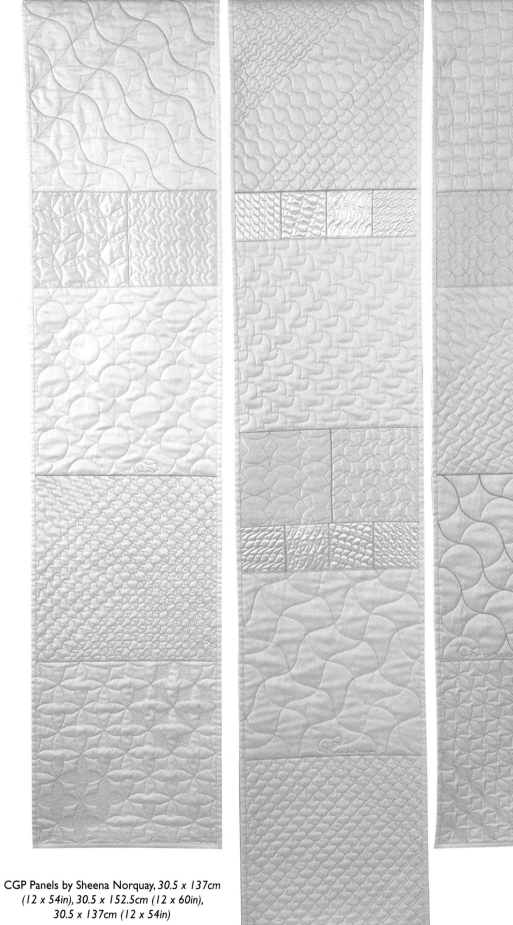

CGP Panels by Sheena Norquay, *30.5 x 137cm
(12 x 54in), 30.5 x 152.5cm (12 x 60in),
30.5 x 137cm (12 x 54in)*

Manchester Hexagon Quilt, *224 x 239cm (88 x 94in)*, mid-19th century

The hexagon quilt (opposite), made in the mid-19th century, was found in the Manchester area in northern England. Owned by Helen Stewart Watt of Arbroath, Scotland, who was born in around 1863–64, it is made from printed and plain cottons with double rosettes of hexagons linked by a surrounding row or 'path' of pink and blue hexagons in a pattern sometimes called Grandmother's Flower Garden. At some stage, the quilt was damaged on the right side and it has been rejoined with the loss of part of the second vertical row of rosettes.

Because the hexagon shape tessellates with other hexagons to form a mosaic pattern, it offers various design opportunities. A simple pattern of single rosettes is made from six hexagons placed around a central hexagon. This can be developed into more complex designs such as that shown on the coverlet from c. 1870s (see page 84).

HEXAGON QUILT
DAVINA THOMAS

Intrigued by the hexagon shape and the contrast of paper templates framed by fabric turnings, Davina Thomas used computer software to design her contemporary hexagon quilt, Fragments of Time 1 (right). Scanned images were distorted by warping and twirling; various scales of hexagon shapes and patterns, washed with soft colours, were computer-printed directly on to fabric for the hexagon centres.

DAVINA THOMAS

Davina has two very different skills that she can apply to her quiltmaking; she grew up knowing how to sew and, having worked extensively in IT, can use a computer as a design tool. She tried patchwork when she was about 10 years old and took it up again as a late teenager, making her first quilt for her parents aged 21. Davina took the City and Guilds Embroidery course whilst in full-time employment and then fitted in the Patchwork and Quilting course around maternity leave and in the evenings. After teaching quilting for a time, she is now a contributing editor to a quilting magazine. Davina's preference is for piecing and, if forced to choose one technique, she declares: 'I would be happy to sew half-square triangles for the rest of my life.'

'I would be happy to sew half-square triangles for the rest of my life.'

COMPUTER WORK

Davina claims to have no drawing skills. 'I cannot even draw a square by hand and have to use a computer to line things up. "Doodling" in sketchbooks is not for me because I tend to lose my sketches – my impatient nature is more suited to computer design work where I can change colour or shape very easily at the click of a mouse.'

Since Davina is happiest when sitting at her computer, her research and design work is done this way. She analyses a theme by first looking up words in a dictionary, consulting a thesaurus for variations and researching further information on the Internet. Davina then moves on to a variety of software design programmes using Quilt-Pro for simple block or frame designs, Serif PhotoPlus (other photo-editing programmes can be used) for distorting images, and Serif DrawPlus and PagePlus for yet further drawing and colouring.

The hexagon shape intrigues Davina. She realized that, with a shape of six equal sides, there was

Coverlet, 253 x 278cm (97 x 109in), c.1870, printed cotton

Hexagons

The hexagon is a ubiquitous shape in quiltmaking; it occurs in quilts from the 18th century to the present day, in patchwork from Britain and mainland European countries such as France and the Netherlands, and from North America and Australia. During the British Quilt Heritage Project, nearly 600 items of hexagon patchwork were recorded from a total of 3,967.[1]

An exhibition in 2004 highlighted the significance of the shape in the history of quiltmaking but also showed how difficult it is to ascertain when it was first used in patchwork.[2] The earliest known dated patchwork coverlets (see page 6) do not feature the hexagon and the design of the majority of surviving patchwork from the 18th century is based on the square, with the related half-square triangle being the dominant shape. However, by the end of the 18th century into the 19th century hexagons frequently occur in patchwork coverlets and quilts as seen in the Complex Frame Coverlet 1795–1805 (see pages 11 and 32).

The hexagon is a six-sided geometric shape. When the hexagon sides are of equal length divided by equal angles, it can be grouped geometrically with the equilateral triangle and the diamond, which is made from two equilateral triangles. Such shapes do not combine well with the square and half-square triangle and tend not to be seen together in the same patchwork quilt. The earliest known patchwork to be made from printed cotton, seen in the Levens Hall bed hangings, consists of a mosaic of octagons, crosses, rectangles and long hexagons (the elongation of the shape changes it so that it interlocks with the other two shapes).[3] This long hexagon cannot be grouped geometrically with the standard hexagon. The elongated hexagon shape can also be seen in the Mary Prince Mosaic Coverlet (right). Pieced in printed cottons, the coverlet was probably made in about 1815 even though it is dated and signed 'Mary Prince, 1803'.[4]

The commonest construction technique for hexagon patchwork wraps fabric over paper templates cut to the hexagon shape, with the turnings tacked (basted) to the paper. The fabric or paper hexagon units are oversewn (whip stitched) together by hand and, if desired, the tacking (basting) and papers are then removed. In the past, it seems that the papers were sometimes left in the patchwork. Writing or printing on the papers often provides an intriguing insight into life at the time the patchwork was made.

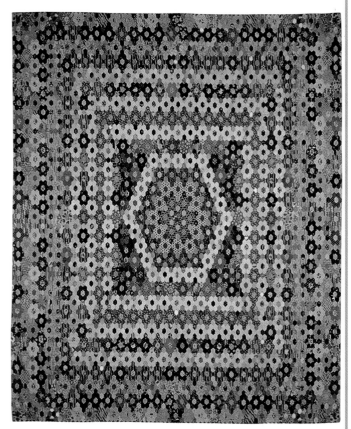

Mary Prince Mosaic Coverlet, *230 x 275cm (91 x 108in), made from long hexagons in plain and printed cotton and linen, c. 1815*

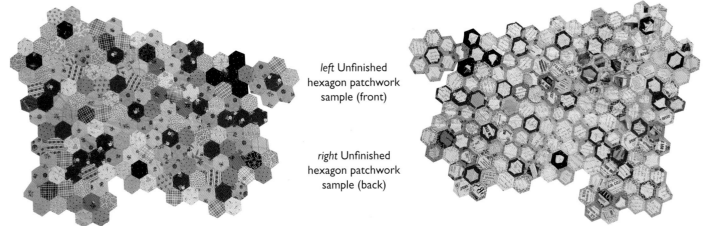

left Unfinished hexagon patchwork sample (front)

right Unfinished hexagon patchwork sample (back)

Distorted computer image of the
Manchester Hexagon Quilt

potential for creating variation by distortion or even making curves on the original straight edges. She says: 'Hexagon quilts appeal to me because so many people know about them. Even people who don't know anything about quilts will recognize a hexagon quilt. I especially like the fact that so many have the papers left in and these give us clues to the people and the households that made them.'

Davina used images of the Manchester Hexagon Quilt and unfinished hexagon patchwork samples also from The Quilters' Guild Collection for this project. She scanned the images and the front and back of the actual samples into her computer. She likes the effect on the back of hexagon patchwork created by piecing fabric over paper hexagon shapes, particularly when the papers have not been removed. 'The samples I used had papers from a seed catalogue. I was quite distracted trying to track down some of the vegetables!' There is a contrast between

the paper template and the surrounding fabric, which is folded-over as a turning. The fabric acts as a frame to the paper in the middle of the shape. Davina linked that frame effect to the framing of the double rosettes by the darker cotton hexagons in the Manchester Hexagon Quilt and felt that it should be an important part of her design.

Distorted computer image of the hexagon
patchwork sample, shown on page 85

'CLICK OF A MOUSE'

Scanned images can be distorted using photo-editing software. Firstly, Davina tried distorting the image of the complete Manchester Hexagon Quilt, but the effects were too extreme. Better results were obtained with larger-scale images of the unfinished hexagon samples, which produced very interesting shapes when warped and twirled. Davina obtained her basic design by distorting an image of the back of one of the unfinished hexagon samples. It was printed off and traced on to white paper over a light box, marking both the edges of the distorted hexagon shapes and the frames created by the fabric turnings. Then the tracing was scanned back into the computer for further design work.

Computer image of the basic design
showing seam lines and turnings traced
from the distorted patchwork sample

left Computer image of the back of the unfinished hexagon patchwork sample with a blue orange overlay

right Computer image of the Manchester Hexagon Quilt with diagonal colourwash

Using Serif PagePlus, Davina added a transparent layer over the top of all the images (original and distorted) and experimented with colour to give a gentle colourwash effect. Such experiments help give a feel for the colour schemes that could be used for a design much more quickly than colouring with paint or pencil. Davina chose dark framing coupled with colourwash effect centres, so she filled the scanned and traced design with multicoloured hexagons and added a dark border.

COMPUTER-GENERATED FABRIC

Davina wanted to use hexagons in different scales for the fabric in the centres of the distorted hexagon shapes in her quilt. The experiments with colourwashes over scanned images provided coloured designs that could be computer printed directly on to cloth. She used the technique described below, but it should be noted that this technique is relatively new and nothing is yet known about how light fast the print will be in the long term.

COMPUTER PRINTING ON TO FABRIC

Quilters can print designs on to fabric by using a home computer and printer together with a product that makes printer ink wash-proof.

YOU WILL NEED
Pre-washed 100 per cent cotton
   or silk fabric
Large tray, such as a cat litter tray
Bubble Jet Set 2000 liquid
Freezer paper

METHOD
1. Cut a strip of fabric to either the length or the width of the sheets of paper that go through your computer printer.
2. Place the end of the fabric in the tray and pour Bubble Jet Set over the fabric until it is damp.

3. Fold down more fabric into the tray to create another layer and pour over more Bubble Jet Set. Continue folding and pouring until all the fabric is folded into the tray and is damp.
4. Hang fabric to dry. If it is folded over a line, the fold line will probably not take colour during the printing process.
5. When dry, cut the fabric to fit the size of paper suitable for the printer and iron it on to freezer paper cut to the same size using a medium to hot iron.

6. To use it in the computer printer, add one fabric/paper sheet at a time (with the fabric on the print side) to avoid jamming and stand by in case of problems. You may need to help the paper through the printer. The simplest printers (where the fabric goes in at the back and comes out of the front with only a slight turn) are the best for this technique. Print off the required images.
7. Leave the fabric to dry for 30 minutes and then peel off the freezer paper. Wash the fabric in hot water with detergent, then dry and iron it.

Computer image of the basic design infilled with coloured hexagons and dark frames

TO THE SEWING MACHINE

Davina was able to scale up the traced design to eight-page poster size on her computer and this established the final size of the quilt. The print of the scaled-up design became the pattern for the quilt and was used to trace off freezer paper templates for both the hexagon centres and the framed hexagon shapes. 'The six-sided hexagon shape is very difficult to 'square up', so I chose to leave the edges of the quilt uneven. I felt that the quilt needed a diagonal feel to its bottom edge but decided to leave this decision until the main part of the quilt was completed.'

The quilt was constructed using a Log Cabin technique to sew the frames on to the hexagon centres. The computer-printed fabric was used for the centres and white cotton, coloured with Pebeo Transparent Fabric paint, was used for the fabric strips that made up the frames. The Log Cabin strips, joined to the hexagon centres, were trimmed to fit the templates for the framed hexagon shapes before the shapes were joined together. Davina scanned a photograph of the main part of the quilt into the computer and experimented with adding further hexagons along the bottom to get the desired diagonal edge. She then made more framed hexagons and added them to the quilt.

Davina finished the quilt with simple machine quilting outlining the hexagons. She stiffened the uneven edges of the quilt with thick non-woven interfacing such as Craft Vilene (Pellon), slip stitched into the inside of the quilt. The back of the quilt was made from computer-printed fabric with images taken from various stages of the design process.

'Although I had used these design techniques on previous projects, working with the hexagon shape was a new departure – one that I would like to pursue, though perhaps on a design with less complex piecing.'

Computer image of the experiment with adding hexagons to the bottom edge

Fragments of Time 1 by Davina Thomas, *53 x 92cm (21 x 36in)*

Silk Triangles Coverlet, *100 x 128cm (39 x 50in),* from the second half of the
19th century, made by Mary Dennis of Hartland, Devon, in silks

The colourful Silk Triangles Coverlet (opposite) has had a chequered life. Originally a bed cover made by Mary Dennis of Hartland, Devon, in the second half of the 19th century, it was later reduced to one-quarter of its size and edged with a wide band of crocheted lace, possibly to make a table cover. The coverlet consists of multicoloured silk equilateral triangles in rows of dark and light colours. The variation of colours along the rows, creating random larger triangles where the colour contrast is low, gives an interesting tonal effect and makes the coverlet 'sparkle'.

MOSAIC QUILT
BARBARA WEEKS

Inspired by the shapes of the Silk Triangles Coverlet (opposite), and the movement and texture of modern glass buildings, Barbara Weeks created her quilt re: Swiss (right). She dyed silk fabric using salt and wax resist methods, before bonding them on to tear-away stabilizer. With black as a foil, sheer fabrics echoed the transparency of glass and more texture was added with machine stitching and tucks.

'The majority of my recent work has been with bonded appliqué, using repeated shapes, mosaic-style and dense machine quilting.'

30 St Mary Axe, the London headquarters of Swiss Re

BARBARA WEEKS

Barbara grew up knowing how to sew and used this skill as a basis for a teaching career, teaching stitched textiles in secondary schools and later, patchwork and quilting in adult education. As a well-known teacher and City and Guilds verifier, she sometimes has to find a balance between teaching commitments and her desire to design and make her own quilts.

Barbara made her first patchwork item, a suede patchwork waistcoat, whilst at college, but her real interest in quilting began in the 1980s when she took a number of workshops with leading quilters, including Pauline Burbidge, Susan Denton and Linda Straw. She says: 'I can still see their influences in my work. I enjoy relating most traditional techniques to contemporary methods, but the majority of my recent work has been with bonded appliqué, using repeating shapes, mosaic-style and dense machine quilting. Patterning cloth by dyeing and texturing is also important.'

SIMPLE GEOMETRIC SHAPES

Barbara was attracted to the Silk Triangles Coverlet because of 'the lasting appeal of simple geometric shapes. In many of these [old] quilts, the colours have faded, but here there is a strong contrast, including black, which is effective and timeless.' The appeal of such shapes has led Barbara to mosaic tiling in Roman floors or Gaudi's buildings in Barcelona and to contemporary use of repeated shapes, especially in glass roofs and walls, such as the hexagon at the Eden Project, Cornwall, the triangle in the Great Court at the British Museum, London, and 30 St Mary Axe, the London headquarters of Swiss Re in the City of London.

In a flat quilt, the shapes repeat in a regular pattern, but when used over the surface of a building, the straight-edged shapes can give the illusion of a curve. Barbara's studies of contemporary buildings highlighted the movement created by these 'curves', enhanced by reflections in the glass. Bringing together the past and the contemporary, Barbara chose to combine the feel of repeat triangles and contrasting colours in the Silk Triangles Coverlet with the impression of movement and texture achieved by modern glass buildings.

30 ST MARY AXE

A 40-storey tower, nicknamed 'The Gherkin', has recently become a feature on the London city landscape. This cigar-shaped tower, totally clad in triangles and diamonds of glass, reflecting the seasons and weather as well as the surrounding buildings, became the basis of Barbara's contemporary take on repeating triangles.

Barbara begins her design process with photography and sketching, using painting, printing and paper collage exercises to draw out features that give the

Mosaic Patchwork

The facility to tessellate simple geometric shapes to form a mosaic has always been a major factor in patchwork. Triangles, diamonds, octagons, pentagons, squares, rectangles and hexagons combine into simple repeating patterns, as seen in the Silk Triangles Coverlet or the silk Tumbling Blocks pattern coverlet made in about 1890 (right). The three-dimensional effect of the Tumbling Blocks is achieved by clever and consistent working of three tones of dark, medium and light. More complex patterns can be seen in the complex frame quilt, made between 1795–1805 (see pages 11 and 32).

Traditionally, Mosaic patchwork is made by wrapping fabric over paper templates and oversewing (whip stitching) the units together. This technique is time-consuming, but, for shapes such as the hexagon or more complex figurative patchwork designs (as seen in the earliest dated patchwork, the 1718 Silk Patchwork Coverlet shown on page 7), it is the best way to achieve accurate piecing. Currently there is some debate about what this technique should be called. It is often referred to as 'paper template piecing', but this can cause confusion with foundation piecing, which can also utilize paper. Sometimes the name given is 'English' patchwork, which would restrict the technique to one country. Research suggests that the technique did evolve in Europe and that the oldest dated patchwork is indeed British, but this way of making patchwork occurs all over the world. So, the term 'Mosaic patchwork' has come to be used.

Mosaic patchwork has been made in Britain from at least the early 18th century and continues to the present day. It was sewn in mainland Europe and early settlers and visitors took the technique to North America and to other countries with a British influence, such as Australia. Studies of quilts in Charleston Museum, South Carolina, USA, reveal that this method was popular with needlewomen in that area by the early 19th century, although other piecing techniques became more popular in the USA during the 19th century.[1] In the mid-19th century, Mosaic patchwork was reintroduced to the US as a novelty technique for silk patchwork, by American ladies' magazines drawing upon styles seen in Britain.[2]

During the second half of the 19th century, Mosaic patchwork made from silks and velvets was popular with women who could afford luxurious fabrics and had the leisure time to pursue sewing as a hobby. At this time, the diamond, triangle and hexagon were the popular shapes.

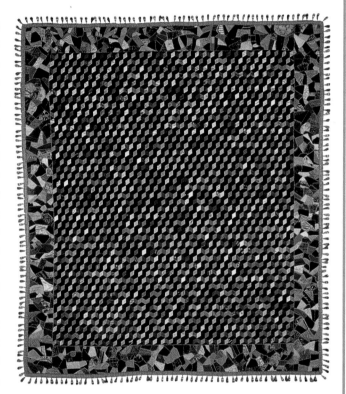

Silk and velvet coverlet, *198 x 221cm (78 x 87in)*, with Tumbling Blocks centre and Crazy patchwork border, made by Catherine Jarvis Briggs (born in Devon 1856), c. 1890

essential feel of the topic. In her study of the Swiss Re headquarters, she was 'drawn to the effects of reflection on the glass panels and intrigued by the internal structural features of the building that can be seen in glimpses through the windows'. The exterior of the building is patterned by sections of darker coloured glass that spiral up the building, enhancing the curved effect. 'A series of sketches studying the curved shapes and tonal arrangements led me to consider using a transparent section to echo the glass in the final quilt.'

Images from Barbara's sketchbook: colour sketch of the top of 30 St Mary Axe; printed impression of the triangles

Paper collage in triangles emphasizing the observed colour and texture of the glass in the tower

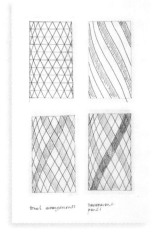

Section of triangles showing tonal arrangements

One of the sketches had sufficient tonal variation to give a feeling of movement across the design. Using the winter blues and greens from her images of the tower, Barbara coloured it first in watercolour pencils and then, in her final colour design, using paper collage. 'I used a variety of patterned and textured papers in the collage to try to reproduce the patterns on the glass windows caused by a combination of external reflections and internal structure. I realized that the curved effect in the design would be very subtle. Once the design was scaled up using a photocopier, the effect could only be seen by viewing it from further away like a picture on a wall.' Barbara likes to transfer her full-scale design to tear-away stabilizer, numbering all the components for future reference. She pins this to her wall and will check it frequently during the construction stage.

'The Silk Triangles Coverlet inspired me to use black as a foil to the blue and green colours derived from studies of the Swiss Re headquarters. I decided to use the bonded appliqué method for the quilt, with stitching and dyeing techniques to reproduce the textures.'

TEXTURE IN CLOTH

Working with the basic triangle design from her study, Barbara experimented with manipulated texture by stitching, making tucks and gathering fabric. Some effects were too fussy, but others, such as double needle and random stitching, and making tucks, gave the effect she was seeking. 'I like to work with silk, so chose silk habotai, crêpe de chine, organza and a semi-sheer fabric with a strong weave to provide a variety of fabric textures. To further enhance the textures, I dyed the silks using steam-fixed silk paints and wax resist and salt effects, and applied extra colour using fusible web such as Bondaweb.'

A TRANSPARENT PANEL

Barbara wanted to echo the transparent property of glass in her project and found she could do this by using sheer fabrics. 'Using silk organza, which I had dyed and textured, I wanted to create a translucent strip running diagonally through the quilt; viewed with front light only it would appear like the rest of the quilt, but when lit from the side or back it would change character.' This translucent panel could create problems during construction: the strip had to be strong to prevent distortion when the quilt was hung. Working with trial samples, Barbara found that quilting two layers of silk organza together using a double needle provided enough body and the panel would be stable if the translucent triangles were mounted on to the wadding (batting) and backing fabric, with a window cut through them, before the top of the quilt was added.

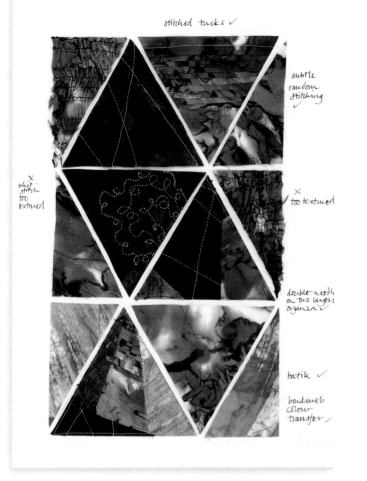

Handwritten annotations on image:
stitched tucks ✓
subtle random stitching
X whip stitch too textured
X too textured
double needle on two layers again
batik ✓
bondaweb colour transfer ✓

Experiments with stitched texture

Textured silk fabric using Bondaweb colour transfer

Final design in paper collage

TEXTURING CLOTH

SALT EFFECTS ON PAINTED SILK
Interesting patterns can be produced on painted silk fabric by sprinkling coarse salt over it whilst the silk paint is still wet. The salt helps to concentrate the colour in the paint on some areas. Once the paint and salt are dry, the salt is brushed off before fixing.

WAX RESIST ON SILK HABOTAI
Apply hot batik wax in random strokes using a brush or crumpled kitchen paper. Do not apply it too thickly or too evenly – the coverage should vary. When the wax is set, dampen the silk and then crumple it to crack the wax. Apply silk paint with a pipette or dropper.

Barbara used a mix of colours to enhance the textured effect.

BONDAWEB COLOUR TRANSFER
Further pattern can be applied to dyed and painted cloth by using Bondaweb and a variety of coloured media.

YOU WILL NEED
Fusible web such as Bondaweb
Colour media such as Markal Artists
    Paintstik, acrylic paint such as
    Liquitex Concentrated Artist
    Colour or silk paint
Fabric such as silk
Parchment paper or similar

METHOD
1. Brush or sponge paint or apply paint stick in random strokes to the adhesive web side of the fusible web. Note that the other side is backed with paper.
2. Allow the paint to dry.
3. Protect all surfaces and any fabric that is not to be coloured with parchment paper or similar. With the paper side of the fusible web uppermost, iron the coloured side on to the fabric.
4. Peel the paper away to reveal the bonded colour on the fabric. The adhesive in the fusible web is still present and it must be covered when ironing the fabric subsequently.

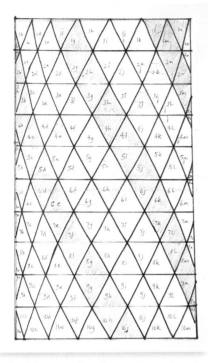

Final design with each triangle numbered
for construction reference

CONSTRUCTION

Appliqué using a fusible material was Barbara's preferred construction method. She used her full-scale design as a guide to trace off the triangles on to a tear-away stabilizer, numbering each triangle as she worked. These became the foundation for piecing individual triangles using her stitched and dyed silks. 'My colour design collage is my guide for the selection of fabric for each triangle, but I make spontaneous changes as the quilt is built up.' Once happy with the colour and tone for all the triangles, Barbara removed the tear-away stabilizer and bonded the triangles to the black quilt top using Bondaweb. The top, wadding (batting) and backing were sandwiched together, a window over the translucent panel was cut into the top and the frames around the translucent triangles were neatened on the back and front.

Barbara chose to maintain the continuity of the design by quilting using a double needle (she has worked some of the textured triangles and translucent panel in this way). Using coloured thread to stand out against the black of the quilt frame, she quilted in broken horizontal lines across the quilt, working occasional triangular sections to further interrupt the linear quilting.

FUTURE PLANS

'This project has inspired me to work with black and translucent fabrics. I have developed ideas from re: Swiss to produce a commission for The Quilters' Guild's new Contemporary Collection combining the triangular mosaic of re: Swiss with a large area of black with translucent triangles cut into it as windows.'

above Detail of re: Swiss showing
transparent panel and stitching

right re: Swiss by Barbara Weeks, backlit
to reveal the transparent panel

re: Swiss by Barbara Weeks, 95 x 139cm (37½ x 54½in)

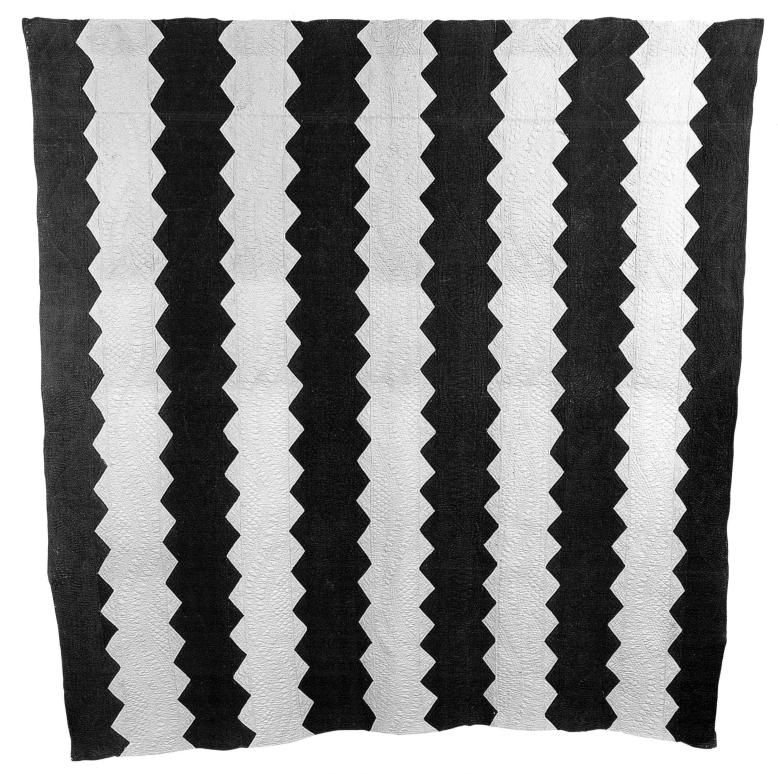

Sawtooth Strippy Quilt, *212 x 200cm (83½ x 79in)*, late 19th century

Although the Sawtooth Strippy Quilt (opposite) is slightly worn, its place in any collection would be justified by the striking and unusual strippy design in a contrasting red and white colour scheme, coupled with exquisite hand quilting. It probably dates from the late 19th century and was made in northern England. Measuring 212 x 200cm (83 x 79in), the quilt has 11 strips of red and white cotton, with a sawtooth row of triangles forming an edge to the strips. The dense quilting has a pattern of large leaf shapes, together with a leaf and stalk motif on the red strips and an undulating wavy line or worm pattern with feather infill on the white.

STRIPPY QUILT
LAURA KEMSHALL

Laura Kemshall works very intuitively. Having filled her sketchbook with studies to reflect the style and proportions of strippy quilts, she experimented with a leaf and stalk motif using appliqué and stencilling techniques. She then felt ready to 'go for it', creating Straight and Narrow (right) using the fold resist dyeing method, which captured the essence of a strippy quilt.

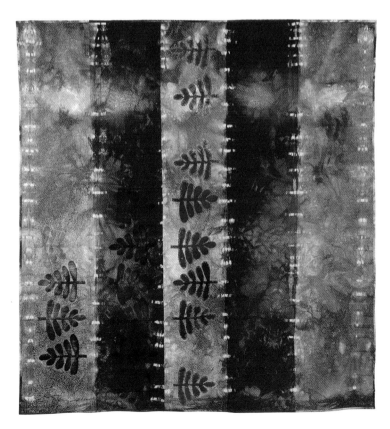

'My work is inspired by a sense of time and space, and the countryside around my home.'

Surrounded by Laura Kemshall,
200 x 300cm (79 x 118in)

Pages from Laura's sketchbook: painted red stripes with cut out 'feathered edging'

LAURA KEMSHALL

Laura describes herself as an artist. She grew up surrounded by quilts and embroidery, and was drawn to quilting because of its tactile nature. However, she feels that she is divided between the fine art and textile worlds, and has ended up with 'a foot in both camps'. For the moment, her artistic talents are being applied to working with fabric and thread, but her ambitions to be an independent artist fed by constant experimentation and the search for inspiration could lead her in exciting new directions in the future.

Laura took a BA course in textiles in which she 'followed the embroidery route in the course'. Since graduating in 2000, Laura has devoted herself to developing her own style and has produced an impressive collection of quilts. She is attracted to an ever-changing list of artists who impress her (a current inspiration is the sculptor Anthony Gormley), but she does not want to repeat what has been done before. 'My work is inspired by a sense of time and space, and the countryside around my home in south Staffordshire.' She made her mark in the quilt world in 2001 by winning an international quilt competition and she has followed this up with many awards since. For the moment, teaching and lecturing are part of Laura's life; she has a full diary of bookings and also works with her mother, Linda Kemshall, teaching online.

WORKING FROM NATURE

Laura says that drawing is at the heart of her work. 'I always work into sketchbooks by drawing, painting and printing anything that inspires me and constantly use a camera to record colours and shapes. Recent work was led by the shape and form of plants, trees and flowers. Beginning with photographic images, I use painting and printing techniques to reproduce or just give an impression of selected parts of an image, until something from all the work catches my eye.' A recent series of quilts evolved from studies of poppies and poppy seed heads, and Laura has now moved on to quilts based on research into hedges.

Many of Laura's quilts have a linear quality with strong vertical lines running through the design either in the background or as plant stems, such as those of the poppy or lily. Her quilt Surrounded (left) is designed to reflect hedges and 'is intended to recreate the sense of being surrounded by them – at one moment forbidding, at the other protective'. It is displayed as an installation, held off the ground by sticks that are an integral part of the design, with one side coming forward and then curving back towards the rest of the quilt. Metamorphosis (shown on page 103) is two quilts in one with four vertical flaps running the length of the quilt: if buttoned to one side, the quilt is based on Laura's research into hedges, if buttoned the other way, then poppy seed heads become visible.

Strippy Quilts

Strippy quilts can be found in both the north of England, where the majority can be seen, and in Wales. They were made in the 19th century (particularly the second half) and in the early 20th century, and they survive in areas where there was a strong tradition of wholecloth quilting.

Strippy quilts are made of alternating coloured strips (generally an odd number), which run down the length of the quilt. In some strippies from Wales, the strips run across the width of the quilt. The strips of cloth are mostly machine sewn together, but the quilts are hand quilted in a strip or, as generally seen in Wales, in a framed quilting layout. This type of quilt is simple to make since large pieces of cloth are sewn together in strips with no complex piecing. Also, the border quilting patterns that run down the strips are easy to plan and to sew in one run, particularly if the quilt is set up lengthwise in a quilting frame.

Oral history back to the early 20th century and observations made by the quilt historian Mavis FitzRandolph just after World War II indicate that the strippy quilt was the most common style made in the north east of England. It is estimated that they accounted for up to 75 per cent of all quilts made during that period. However, far fewer strippies survive to the present day when compared with wholecloth quilts. The discrepancy between the observed frequency of strippy quilt manufacture and the numbers that survive suggests that the strippy quilt can be regarded as the everyday functional quilt, which was quick and comparatively cheap to make, and consequently used until it wore out. During the same period, the wholecloth quilt tended to be made with good quality cotton sateen and was regarded as 'best', many surviving still in good condition, or even unused, in drawers and airing cupboards.

The origin of the strippy quilt is uncertain. Three dated quilts with both strip piecing and strip quilting have been recorded from the 1850s and predate the era when the strippy tops were pieced by sewing machine.[2] Earlier quilts have been recorded with a strippy quilting layout unrelated to their frame-pieced tops.[3] Examples of quilts with strippy tops made of plain strips or alternating pieced and plain strips, but with unrelated quilting, also survive. The period later in the 19th century and into the 20th century sees the development of the 'classic' strippy quilt, but the makers at this time were building upon a traditional quilt style that was already established in Britain.

Strippy quilt, 210 x 230cm (82½ x 90½in) c. 1910
in pink and white cottons

USING THE STRIPPY AS A DESIGN SOURCE

Nature provides boundless inspiration for Laura, so starting with a study of other quilters' work is unusual for her, though she did find echoes of her own work in the vertical feel of strippy quilts. 'I filled my sketchbook with details of strippy quilts, getting a feel for their style and the number and proportions of the strips. Moving to the Sawtooth Strippy, I sketched in pencil and used red and white paints to try to represent the striped effect of the quilt and the jagged effect of the sawtooth edge.' Tracings of the quilting patterns were added and over-painted with red and white.

Laura tried reproducing the sawtooth edge of the strips by experimenting with prairie points. Prairie points are made by folding a square of fabric in half diagonally and then in half again. They are often used to add a jagged edge to a quilt

Sawtooth and Feathered Strippies

A variation of the standard strippy style has the addition of rows of half-square triangles down the sides of the strips to create a jagged effect. When the long side (hypotenuse) of the triangle is joined to the strip, the pattern seen in the Sawtooth Strippy Quilt is created. Sewing one of the shorter sides of the triangle to the strip creates a design described by quilters as 'feathered'.

The use of triangles in either way in strippy quilts is unusual. During the British Quilt Heritage Project, very few of either variation were documented and Dorothy Osler's study of the classic strippy quilt does not include this feature.[4] Feathered designs are seen in frame or block patterns, often associated with star or square on point designs, and are also widely recorded in North America. In the United States, a feathered strippy patchwork pattern called, amongst other names, Tree Everlasting, is well known so there is speculation about the origins of this pattern.[5]

Detail of the Sawtooth Strippy Quilt showing the quilting

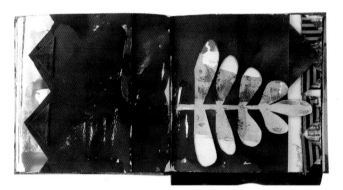

Pages from Laura's sketchbook: cut paper leaf
and stalk motif with prairie points

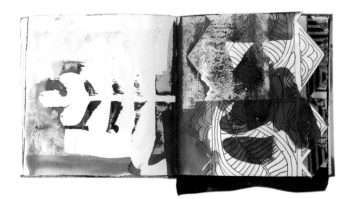

Pages from Laura's sketchbook: quilting design from the
Sawtooth Strippy Quilt over-painted in red and white

but can also be inserted into seams in the body of a quilt. 'I rejected the experiment because the points were too fussy. Attracted to the quilting motifs, particularly the leaf and stalk motif, I worked samples of this motif using appliqué techniques and experimented with stencilling over a paper cut-out of the shape.'

GOING FOR IT

Laura reaches a point when she feels that her research is done and she is confident 'to go for it with cloth', working with a developing design whilst she is actually making the quilt. 'For this project, rather than piecing together red and white cloth in strips, I decided to create the strippy design by dyeing cotton cloth in a red dye using a resist dyeing method. Once I saw the effect of this, I planned to add applied, stencilled and quilted leaf and stalk motifs flowing diagonally across the quilt.'

DYEING THE STRIPS

The fabric for Laura's quilt was fold resist-dyed as a single piece, one strip wider than the finished quilt using a cold-water fibre reactive dye. To obtain the strip effect, Laura folded the cotton in half and then lengthwise into three concertina folds in each half to create six sections. Wooden clothes pegs, placed at intervals along the long sides, held the folds in place (see diagram below right); this resulted in the attractive effect of white areas seen on the finished quilt. The cotton on the outer folds was dyed darker than that on the inner folds. She says: 'The dye just travels through the fabric and the results are down to serendipity a lot of the time. I dyed two fabrics for the quilt and chose the best one with the clearest stripes.' Laura cut out the stripe with the least contrast and sewed the fabric back together to create the remaining five strips (an odd number is a feature of strippy quilts).

The middle, light strip has a line of reverse appliqué leaf and stalk motifs. On the strips next to the middle one, the same motifs are created by painting over freezer paper stencils using Markal Artists Paintstiks (Shiva). The paint sticks are very easy to use on cotton, but the paint should be left to dry for a few days afterwards to avoid smudging.

Metamorphosis by Laura Kemshall, *100 x 100cm (39 x 39in)*

Pages from Laura's sketchbook showing: *left* red quilted cotton over-painted with white emulsion paint; *right* sample of reverse appliqué in cotton

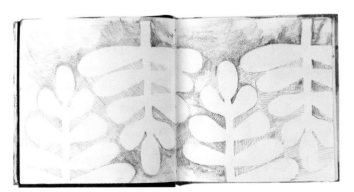

Pages from Laura's sketchbook: the stencilled leaf and stalk motif

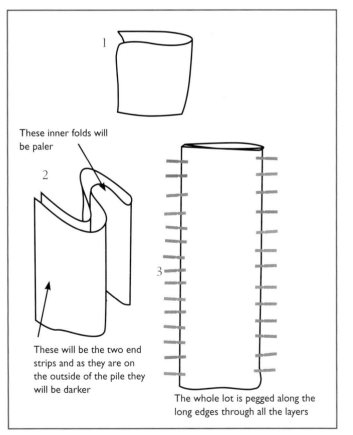

1

These inner folds will be paler

2

3

These will be the two end strips and as they are on the outside of the pile they will be darker

The whole lot is pegged along the long edges through all the layers

Folding cloth for resist dyeing

Resist Dyeing

Resist dyeing has a long and ancient tradition, going back to the blue dyes, indigo and woad, which are used without mordants and are slow to penetrate cotton fibres. For centuries, this characteristic has been exploited to create pattern without the use of printed mordants. There are many methods of treating or manipulating cloth to create a barrier to dyes, resulting in areas of undyed (resisted) cloth in contrast to the fully dyed background.

In a number of countries, substances such as wax, clay, resin and starch pastes were used to provide a physical barrier for resist dyeing on cotton. European textile printers refined the resist techniques and produced many recipes for resist pastes (or reserves) containing substances such as pipe-clay, starch, wax and egg white to provide a physical resist and chemicals such as sulphate of copper and sulphuric acid to 'throw off' the dye from the protected areas.[6] The pastes were applied in a thick liquid form by hand painting or block printing on to the cloth. Then they were dried and hardened so that the fibres were coated thoroughly before the cloth was dyed. The resisted areas remained undyed whereas the rest of the cloth acquired the colour of the dye that was in the dye bath.

An alternative way of protecting areas of cloth from the dye is to manipulate the cloth so that the dye cannot reach the fibres. Known collectively in Japan as shibori, two different resist methods are widely used in Asia and Africa. Tie-dye involves knotting, folding, binding or tying the cloth, often wrapping it around small beads or stones before tying. The other method is stitch resist, where the cloth is hand or machine stitched and gathered tightly before being immersed in the dye bath. Unlike the resist method using pastes or wax, which give precise patterns, these methods are less predictable and the patterns incorporate areas of subtle shading because of the variability of the dye penetration.

Contemporary textile artists frequently use tie-dye and stitch resist techniques in their work. Modern dyes such as cold-water fibre reactive dyes penetrate cotton fibres very easily and the effects achieved can be different from those achieved when using indigo. Often there is a lower level of contrast between the dyed and resisted areas.

Outline quilting further enhances the motifs. Laura finished the quilt with hand seeding around the motifs and free machine quilting in a jagged style on the background cloth. The contrast between the red and white strips was emphasized with vertical machine quilting lines outlining the clothes peg marks.

By applying her own design methods and preferred sewing techniques to traditional ideas, Laura has created a quilt that, whilst having the essence of the original inspiration, is very much in her own style.

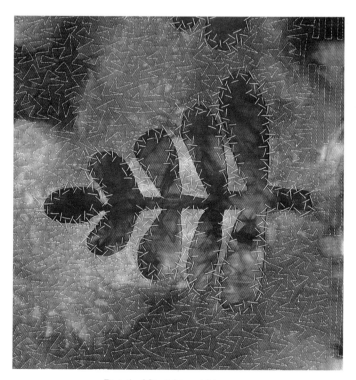

Detail of Straight and Narrow

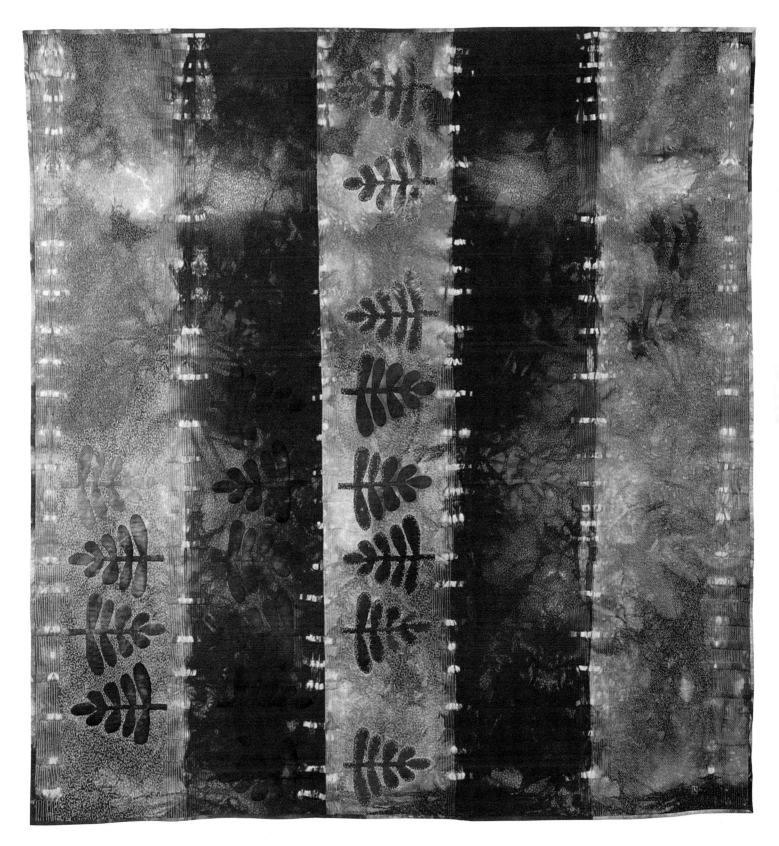

Straight and Narrow by Laura Kemshall, *132 x 140cm (52 x 55in)*

Tree of Life Coverlet, *305 x 305cm (120 x 120in)*, in cotton and linen, late 18th to early 19th century

The unknown needlewoman who made this coverlet (opposite) at the very beginning of the 19th century has produced a stunning example of an appliquéd and embroidered coverlet in the style known as Broderie Perse. It is made from white linen with a variety of large-scale printed linens and cottons applied in the central design of a tree and flowers – a motif often described as the Tree of Life. A number of floral borders surround the tree. The generous size of this coverlet means it would have covered a very large bed.

BRODERIE PERSE BAGS

MELYN ROBINSON

Broderie Perse appealed to Melyn Robinson because of its exotic quality, but she found that only traditional fabric designs had the large, well-defined shapes she needed to create her bags. She used photocopies of the fabrics, to design her free-edged Broderie Perse Evening Bags.

MELYN ROBINSON

Melyn learned to sew at a young age, when growing up in the USA. Her mother was a needlepoint designer, so she 'grew up with "try your own designs" as the norm'. She liked drawing, but found painting difficult and took to quiltmaking when she came to England as an alternative way to create designs and pictures without 'the interference of the paintbrush'.

Melyn usually works out a whole design for a quilting project on graph paper, photocopying it several times and trying a number of colour ideas using watercolour paint, coloured pencils or coloured paper cut from magazines. Broderie Perse appealed to Melyn because of its exotic quality, but she realized that the specific technique and the need to use a large-scale printed fabric with definite colours and motifs dictated a different approach to the design process – graph paper was not needed here.

'I found myself drawn to hand appliqué, using both hand-dyed and commercial fabric in rich colours.'

FASHION CHANGES

High-quality linen and cotton fabrics were used for the appliqué on the Tree of Life Coverlet. The fabrics are printed furnishings that were both fashionable and expensive in the early 19th century, not the utilitarian fabric that cotton later became. At this time, Broderie Perse was worked using fabrics with the flower, leaf and tree designs that had been influenced by imported Asian textiles of the 17th and 18th centuries.

When choosing fabric to explore designs, Melyn found that she had a limited choice of modern larger-scale prints with defined motifs. 'My choice was to use either contemporary printed fabric with smaller motifs or more traditional fabric designs with larger shapes, using the motifs in a different way.'

above Traditional and contemporary designed fabric

A PHOTOCOPIER AS DESIGN TOOL

Though these limitations of technique and printed fabric introduced problems, Melyn feels that Broderie Perse is a good method for someone who is not yet confident in creating original designs. 'For a new quilt designer, the limitations can be an advantage.'

'I used a photocopier to copy a number of printed fabrics in both black and white and colour formats. I then cut out motifs and played around with them, trying a number of different combinations of shapes in various orientations by sticking them on to actual or photocopied background fabrics or coloured magazine paper.' Melyn describes this as 'a very easy but fun design method'.

Design work with photocopied fabric

Persian Embroidery

Broderie Perse, literally Persian embroidery, is an appliqué method that uses whole motifs of flowers, leaves, trees, birds and animals cut from a number of printed fabrics and applied to a plain fabric to create a new design. The motifs are applied as single or repeat units, or combined with others to create a composite design such as a bouquet of flowers or a tree. This type of composite design makes up the centre of the Tree of Life Coverlet, with branches, stems, flowers and leaves cut from a number of fabrics and assembled on a mound created from further fabrics. The raw edges of the motifs are turned under and sewn with a simple hem stitch; another popular method was to neaten the edges with blanket or herringbone stitch. On this coverlet, further blanket stitch and other embroidery stitches embellish the complete Tree of Life design.

Detail of the Tree of Life Coverlet

CREATING A BAG

Melyn's design work with photocopied fabrics included using paper motifs on various styles of bag with a number of luxurious fabrics as the background cloth. Her playing with designs led to the idea of shapes on and beyond the edge of the bag in what she describes as 'free-edged Broderie Perse'.

She chose two styles – one a simple rectangle with a top opening, the other a fold-over shape with side gussets and flap. The rectangular bag would have motifs applied towards the top and above the top edge of the opening. Broderie Perse appliqué would extend beyond the edge of the flap of the fold-over bag.

Two examples of design work with photocopied fabric

FREE-EDGED APPLIQUE

The fold-over bag was part assembled before the appliqué was worked. Melyn ironed fusible web (such as Bondaweb) to the back of the fabric motifs for both bags and cut them out, allowing about 6mm (¼in) spare

fabric along the edges that would be free of the bags. She then ironed the motifs in place on the bag fabrics and, where a motif protruded beyond the edge, ironed it to thick non-woven interfacing. The interfacing was backed, again using fusible web, with a silky fabric chosen in a colour to suit the appropriate bag. The three layers of motif fabric, interfacing and backing were cut away along the free edges of the motifs. All the edges of the motifs, including those that protruded beyond the edge were machine satin stitched to neaten the edges and stop fraying. Quilters often do the machine satin stitch twice, which gives a neater, more tailored edge. Both bags were made up after the satin stitching had been worked. Decorative stitching and beads were then added.

THE RESULT

Melyn said 'I do not think I have seen Broderie Perse used in quite this way before. The technique originally evolved because the fabrics used were expensive, so I felt it appropriate to use the technique for a small but glitzy bag with silky fabric and beads.'

The Ladies' Work Society Coverlet, *211 x 256cm (83 x 111in)*, made in cotton and linen in the late 19th century.

The Ladies' Work Society Coverlet (opposite), made from blue and off-white linen applied with cotton motifs, is a very elegantly designed piece from the late 19th century. It has a framed layout with plain and appliqué borders of varying widths around a large central area, containing four circles of blue linen enclosing floral and circular motifs and the word 'Industria' embroidered in satin stitch. The appliqué fabrics are good quality printed dress cottons in mauves and greens with some red and blue. All the motifs, circles and borders, are applied to the linen background and the raw edges of fabric are caught down with couched, stranded embroidery silks in mauve, green, blue and cream. On the back is a small woven label with the text 'The Ladies' Work Society 31 Sloane St. London SW' and a coronet.[1]

APPLIQUE QUILT
JANICE GUNNER

Janice Gunner picked up on the flower and leaf motifs in the Ladies' Work Society coverlet (opposite), its colours and its Arts and Crafts style. Instead of intricate handwork, she used machine appliqué techniques to make Setting Seed (right), adding couched cord for extra texture to hand-dyed and painted fabrics to make her contemporary wall hanging.

'I like to add colour to my work by using lots of fabric dyeing, painting and printing.'

Cockscomb Quilt, *215 x 207cm (85 x 82in),
a less sophisticated appliqué cotton quilt
from the late 19th century*

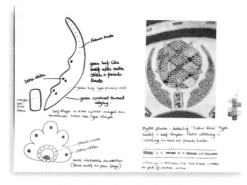

Pages from Janice's sketchbook:
shapes from the coverlet

JANICE GUNNER

Janice has been making quilts for the last 30 years. She loves working with fabric and threads, and was drawn to the colour and texture of quilts. 'I am self taught but was determined to gain a recognizable qualification in quilting by taking the City and Guilds Patchwork and Quilting course in the 1990s and was awarded the first ever Medal for Excellence in patchwork and quilting in 1991.' She has continued to develop her work, achieving a Diploma in Stitched Textiles, and in 1999 was awarded the Jewel Pearce Patterson Scholarship for international quilt teachers.

Janice enjoys colour, looking to artists such as Monet, Klee and Van Gogh for inspiration. 'I like to add colour to my work by using lots of fabric dyeing, painting and printing techniques as well as other textile media such as embroidery for extra texture.'

INSPIRED BY THE ARTS AND CRAFTS STYLE

Artist and designer William Morris is a great favourite of Janice's. 'I love the style of the Arts and Crafts Movement and am constantly drawn to Morris for sources of inspiration, especially his use of colour. This was the main reason why I chose the Ladies' Work Society Coverlet as my design source – it was so unlike the other appliqué quilts I had seen. Most of my work is pieced, so appliqué was a bit different for me. The curved shapes in the coverlet inevitably lent themselves to further appliqué.'

The Ladies' Work Society Coverlet has a sophistication not seen in the more naïve fold and cut (made by folding fabric in half and quarters and cutting designs 'snowflake' style) or floral appliqué quilts of this period, such as in the Cockscomb Quilt (left). Made in the north of England from plain red, green and white cotton, the maker of this quilt could well have been influenced by American appliqué designs of the time.

Janice often initiates the design process with fabric placed directly on to a design wall, but for this project sketches and photographs of the coverlet were the starting point. She drew all the main shapes seen on the coverlet, recording colours of fabric and threads as well as the embroidery embellishment. She liked the stylized floral patterns and focused on the four-petal design in the outer appliqué border. 'I liked this floral type shape, it reminded me of Proteas (flowers from South Africa). The green shape around the rose pattern in the inner circle is very leaf-like and the two provided a good combination.'

FINAL DESIGNS

Janice wanted to keep as much of the feel of the original coverlet as she could in her quilt, choosing the same purple and green colour scheme with a background of blue and off-white vertical bands to echo the frames of the original. 'I used the one flower motif in purple colours shading down from light to dark on a strip of blue, and

The Arts and Crafts Movement and the Ladies' Work Society

Towards the end of the 19th century there was a strong desire amongst many artists to promote architecture and the applied arts as significant artistic disciplines in their own right. In reaction against establishment prejudice towards anything not considered fine art, influential designers such as William Morris and Walter Crane encouraged the development of the Arts and Crafts Movement. They felt that standards of design and workmanship would be improved if craftsmen worked alongside designers and if labour was allied strongly with creativity.

The Movement saw a revival of interest in all handmade crafts and in particular a focus on textile design, including embroidery, with the establishment of a number of ladies' embroidery societies, the most famous being the Royal School of Art Needlework. The Ladies' Work Society, part of this revival, was set up in 1875 under the patronage of Princess Louise, Duchess of Argyll, to provide means of employment for distressed gentlewomen who had few skills apart from school education and fine needlework. Clothing and decorative objects were made to order through the Society and uncommissioned needlework was sold at the Society's premises in London.[2]

At that time the most popular embroidery was Berlin woolwork. Worked on commercially printed canvas using simple tent or cross stitches, the woolwork did not require any design input to make small decorative items such as chair seats or clothing accessories such as slippers. The new styles of embroidery were far looser, with a variety of stitches and greater attention to original design. Appliqué embroidery, often with outline couching threads and surface embellishment, as seen in the Ladies' Work Society Coverlet, became a widely used embroidery technique for followers of the Arts and Crafts Movement.

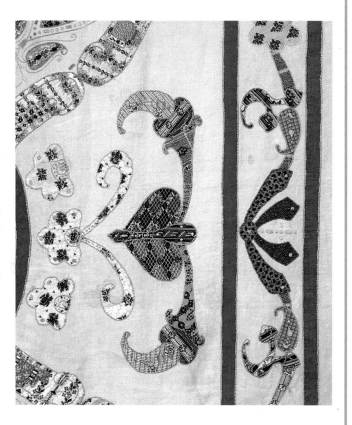

Detail of the Ladies' Work Society Coverlet, showing appliqué motifs and embroidery embellishment

scattered rather than in a formal row. The leaf motif was too smooth on its convex curved side, so I gave it more shape and placed it running down an off-white band.'

Janice wanted to keep the couched thread embellishment around the applied shapes. 'In order to blur the hard edge of the join between the blue and off-white background strips, I added extra couched threads in a 'twisted vine' shape running vertically down the join. Cotton was my choice of fabric for the blue background and the appliqué motifs, with natural linen for the off-white band. I like the effect of hand-coloured cloth, so have included a selection of hand-dyed and painted fabrics. Space dyeing gives the uneven effect I am looking for in some of the fabrics.' Only the ochre yellow centres of the flowers are a commercially printed cotton.

Pages from Janice's sketchbook: flower shapes

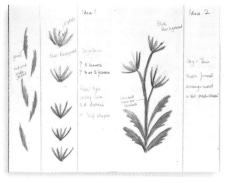

Pages from Janice's sketchbook:
ideas for a design

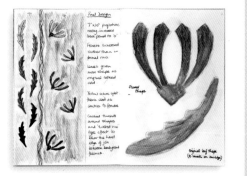

Pages from Janice's sketchbook: final design
with flower and original leaf shapes

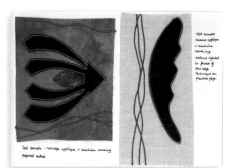

Pages from Janice's sketchbook: samples *left*
raw edge appliqué; *right* reverse appliqué.

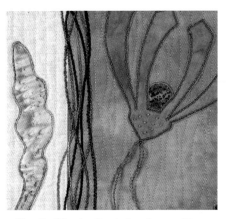

Detail of Setting Seed, showing machine-
couched threads and beads

SPACE DYEING FOR FABRIC AND THREADS

Space dyeing is a method of colouring fabric and threads in a completely random manner. Natural fibres such as cotton, linen, viscose rayon and silk can be dyed with Procion fibre reactive cold-water dyes to achieve unique colour combinations and patterns.

As with all chemicals, these powder dyes must be handled with care. Ensure the room is well ventilated and wear protective clothing, rubber gloves and a face mask. Keep separate utensils and containers for dyeing sessions and protect work surfaces with newspaper. Label the dyes clearly and store them and made-up solutions safely.

YOU WILL NEED
Shallow tray or old washing up bowl
2 empty 1–2 litre (2–4 pint) plastic
    bottles
Empty jam (jelly) jars with screw lids
1kg (35oz) washing soda crystals
1kg (35oz) cooking salt
Procion fibre reactive cold-water dye
Approximately 2m (2yd) pre-washed
    cotton, linen or silk plus threads

METHOD
1. Cut the fabric into 8 or 16 'fat' pieces. Soak the fabric and thread in water until all the fibres have taken up water.
2. To make the dye fix solution, dissolve 100g (3½oz) washing soda in 500ml (18fl oz) hot water. Top up the solution with 500ml (18fl oz) cold water. Store it in a labelled plastic bottle.
3. To make the salt solution, dissolve 150g (5oz) salt in 500ml (18fl oz) hot water and top up the solution with 500ml (18fl oz) cold water. Store it in a labelled plastic bottle.
4. To make the dye solution, measure 50ml (2fl oz) salt solution into a jug. Measure 5ml (1tsp) of dye powder into a jam jar and add a little of this measured salt solution to mix to a paste. Once mixed, add the rest of the measured salt solution, screw on the lid and shake the jar to mix the dye thoroughly. Some dyes mix better with the addition of a little

hand-hot water. Several pots of different dye colours can be made in this way. The dye/salt solution can be stored for about a week.
5. Remove the fabric and thread from the soaking water and squeeze them gently. Place them in the tray or bowl and scrunch them up.
6. When ready to dye, add 50ml (2fl oz) dye fix solution to each dye/salt jar and mix.
7. Spoon the dye mixtures over the fabric and thread at random. Lift them carefully to allow more dye to be added to the bottom layers, but do not stir them around as this will cause the colours to merge and the space-dyed effect will be lost.
8. Leave the fabric and thread for at least 1 hour and longer if possible.
9. When the fabric and thread have been dyed, rinse them in cold water until the water runs clear. Dispose of all the spent dye solution carefully down the sink with running cold water.
10. Wash the fabric and thread in non-biological fabric detergent and rinse them thoroughly until the water again runs clear. Fabric may be machine washed and tumbled dry. Hand wash threads gently to avoid tangles and blot up moisture by wrapping them in an old towel before hanging them up to dry separately. Dry out of direct sunlight to avoid fading.

MACHINE METHODS OF CONSTRUCTION

One of the original ethics of the Arts and Crafts Movement was respect for handwork. Although the Ladies' Work Society Coverlet was entirely handmade, Janice planned to use machine-sewn techniques for her quilt. She tried samples of both machine-sewn standard appliqué with raw edges and reverse appliqué, preferring the effect of the former.

The cords for couching were machine stitched. 'I used a cording foot on my sewing machine and threaded two different yarns or threads through the hole in the foot. To make the cord, I then stitched the yarns together with machine embroidery thread using a narrow, open zigzag. The same foot was used to couch these cords around the edges of the appliqué shapes; the ends of the cords were left hanging on the flower shapes but were threaded through to the back of the work for the leaves. The same was done for the 'twisted vine' embellishment.'

Janice machine quilted her piece in vertical lines using undulating curves for the blue side and straight lines for the linen. She added traditional binding to the edge of the quilt on two sides and used a facing turned to the quilt back on the other two. 'I worked French knots on the base of the flowers and added some seed beads to enhance the yellow centres.'

NAMING THE QUILT

'My design picked up on the flower and leaf motifs seen in the original coverlet. When I finished the quilt and saw the flowers 'floating' on a blue sky, they looked more like ripe seed heads in the air. So I called it Setting Seed.'

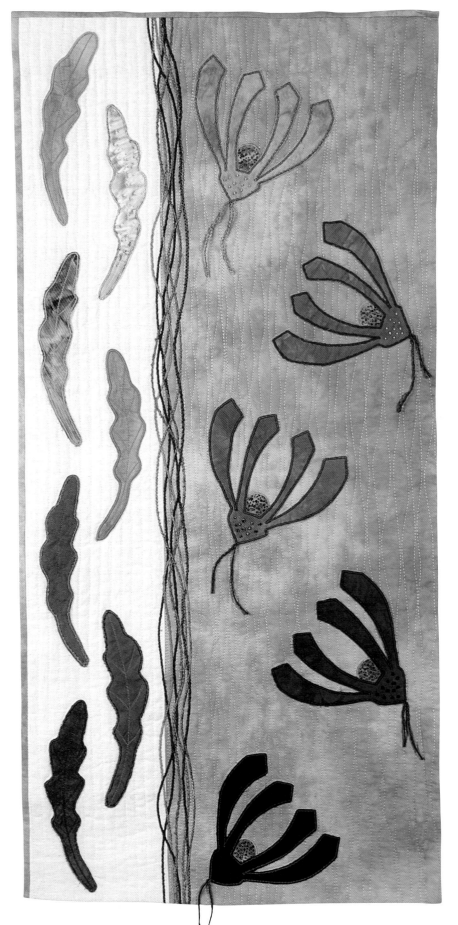

Setting Seed by Janice Gunner, *52 x 107cm (20½ x 42in)*

ENDNOTES

Introduction
1   Michelle Walker (1990) *The Passionate Quilter – Ideas and Techniques from Leading Quilters*. Ebury Press, London, p. 86
2   Janet Rae et al (1995) *Quilt Treasures – The Quilters' Guild Heritage Search*. Deirdre McDonald Books, London

400 Years of Quilts
1   Tina Fenwick Smith and Dorothy Osler (2003) 'The 1718 Silk Patchwork Coverlet: Introduction' in *Quilt Studies* (British Quilt Study Group, Halifax) issue 4/5, p. 28
2   Bridget Long (2003) 'A Comparative Study of the 1718 Silk Patchwork Coverlet' in *Quilt Studies* (British Quilt Study Group, Halifax) issue 4/5, p. 67
3   Mary Hewson (2003) 'The 1718 Silk Patchwork Coverlet: Provenance and Family History' in *Quilt Studies* (British Quilt Study Group, Halifax) issue 4/5, p. 31
4   Deryn O'Connor (2003) 'The Dress Show: A Study of the Fabrics in the 1718 Silk Patchwork Coverlet' in *Quilt Studies* (British Quilt Study Group, Halifax) issue 4/5, p. 79
5   Bridget Long (2003) 'A Comparative Study of the 1718 Silk Patchwork Coverlet' in *Quilt Studies* (British Quilt Study Group, Halifax) issue 4/5, p. 58
6   Sheilah Daughtree (2004) 'Historic Silk Quilted Petticoats' in *Quilt Studies* (British Quilt Study Group, Halifax) issue 6, p. 41
7   Bridget Long (2003) 'A Comparative Study of the 1718 Silk Patchwork Coverlet' in *Quilt Studies* (British Quilt Study Group, Halifax) issue 4/5, p. 63
8   Wendy Hefford (1992) *The Victoria and Albert Museum's Textile Collection Design for Printed Textiles in England from 1750 to 1850*. V&A Publications, London, p. 54
9   Bridget Long (2001) 'Objects of Desire: The Thorne Quilt' in *The Quilter* (The Quilters' Guild of the British Isles, Halifax) issue 86, p. 8
10   Mavis FitzRandolph (1954) *Traditional Quilting: Its Story and its Practice*. Batsford, London, p. 43
11   Christine Stevens (1993) *Quilts*. Dyfed Gomer Press and National Museum of Wales, p. 34
12   Dorothy Osler (1987) *Traditional British Quilts*. Batsford, London, p. 122
13   Ibid, p. 123
14   Ibid, pp. 100, 125, 148
15   Ibid, p. 102
16   Dorothy Osler (2000) *North Country Quilts: Legend and Living Tradition*. Barnard Castle, County Durham, The Bowes Museum and the Friends of The Bowes Museum, p. 50
17   Margaret Tucker (1995) 'The Quiltmakers' in *Quilt Treasures – The Quilters' Guild Heritage Search*. Deirdre McDonald Books, London, p. 141
18   Pauline Adams and Margaret Tucker (1995) 'The Outsiders' in *Quilt Treasures – The Quilters' Guild Heritage Search*. Deirdre McDonald Books, London, p. 156
19   Isobel Holland (2003) 'The Old Guard' in *Popular Patchwork*, November 2003, p. 34
20   Tina Fenwick Smith (2004) 'Averil Colby: A writer ahead of her time' in Textile Perspectives 37 in *The Quilter* (The Quilters' Guild of the British Isles, Halifax) issue 99, p. 6

Frame Quilt
1   Janet Rae (1995) 'In the Frame' in *Quilt Treasures – The Quilters' Guild Heritage Search*. Deirdre McDonald Books, London, p. 17

Red and White Quilt
1   Pauline Adams (2000) 'Objects of Desire – The Red and White Basket Quilt' in *The Quilter* (The Quilters' Guild of the British Isles, Halifax) issue 84, p. 11
2   Tina Fenwick Smith (1999) 'Expansion of the Plain Turkey Red Industry in the Second Half of the Nineteenth Century' in *Quilt Studies* (British Quilt Study Group, Halifax) issue 1, p. 35
3   Yvonne M Khin (1980) *The Collector's Dictionary of Quilt Names and Patterns*. Acropolis Books Ltd, Washington DC, p. 364
4   Deryn O'Connor (1999) 'Four Aspects of Turkey Red: The Process and Early History' in *Quilt Studies* (British Quilt Study Group, Halifax) issue 1, p. 27

Log Cabin Quilt
1   Dinah Travis (1990) *The Sampler Quilt Workbook*. Batsford, London
2   Dinah Travis (1993) *The Appliqué Quilt*. Batsford, London
3   Dinah Travis (1998) *The Miniature Quilt Book*. Batsford, London
4   Janet Rae and Dinah Travis (2004) *Making Connections Around the World with Log Cabin*. RT Publishing, Chartham, Kent
5   Ibid, p. 14
6   Ibid, p. 7

Quilt with a Message
1   Ethel Ewert Abrahams and Rachel K Pannabecker (2000) 'Better Choose Me – Addictions to Tobacco, Collecting and Quilting 1880–1920' in *Uncoverings* (American Quilt Study Group, Lincoln NE) issue 21, p. 79.
2   Janet Rae (1995) 'Why Make a Quilt?' in *Quilt Treasures – The Quilters' Guild Heritage Search*. Deirdre McDonald Books, London, p. 91
3   Rachel Nichols (2004) 'Scripture Quilts from Printed Blocks' in *Quilt Studies* (British Quilt Study Group, Halifax) issue 6, p. 57
4   Ibid, p. 69
5   Dinah Travis (Editor) (2001) *The Nineties Collection*. The Quilters' Guild of the British Isles, Halifax, p. 102

Cord-Quilted Cushion
1   Pauline Adams and Bridget Long (1995) 'Traditions of Quilting' in *Quilt Treasures – The Quilters' Guild Heritage Search*. Deirdre McDonald Books, London, p. 73
2   SFA Caulfield and Blanche C Saward (1882) *The Dictionary of Needlework: An Encyclopaedia of Artistic, Plain and Fancy Needlework*. L Upcott Gill, London, p. 382
3   Avril Hart and Susan North (2000) *Historical Fashion in Detail: The Seventeenth and Eighteenth Centuries*. V&A Publications, London, p.28
4   Clare Rose (2000) 'Quilting in Eighteenth Century London: The Objects, the Evidence' in *Quilt Studies* (British Quilt Study Group, Halifax) issue 2, pp. 11–30
5   Ibid, p. 21
6   Sheila Daughtree (2004) 'Historic Silk Quilted Petticoats' in *Quilt Studies* (British Quilt Study Group, Halifax) issue 6, p. 37
7   Kathryn Berenson (1996) *Quilts of Provence: The Art and Craft of French Quiltmaking*. Thames and Hudson, London
8   Clare Rose (2000) 'Quilting in Eighteenth Century London: The Objects, the Evidence' in *Quilt Studies* (British Quilt Study Group, Halifax) issue 2, p. 25

Crazy Quilt

1   Linda Kemshall (2001) *Colour Moves – Transfer Paints on Fabric*. That Patchwork Place, Bothell WA
2   Penny McMorris (1984) *Crazy Quilts*. EP Dutton, New York
3   Jill Liddell and Yuko Watanabe (1988) *Japanese Quilts*. EP Dutton, New York, p. 17
4   SFA Caulfield and Blanche C Saward (1882) *The Dictionary of Needlework An Encyclopaedia of Artistic, Plain and Fancy Needlework*. L Upcott Gill, London, p. 384
5   Bridget Long (2003) 'A Comparative Study of the 1718 Silk Patchwork Coverlet' in *Quilt Studies* (British Quilt Study Group, Halifax) issue 4/5, pp. 57–60
6   Averil Colby (1958) *Patchwork*. Batsford, London, p. 187

Wholecloth Quilt

1   Dorothy Osler (1998) 'The Quilt Designers of North East England' in *Uncoverings* (American Quilt Study Group, Lincoln NE) issue 19, p. 57
2   Ibid, p. 65
3   Dorothy Osler (2000) *North Country Quilts: Legend and Living Tradition*. Barnard Castle, County Durham, The Bowes Museum and the Friends of The Bowes Museum, p. 28
4   Dorothy Osler (1998) 'The Quilt Designers of North East England' in *Uncoverings* (American Quilt Study Group, Lincoln NE) issue 19, p. 55
5   Mavis FitzRandolph (1954) *Traditional Quilting*. Batsford, London, p. 39
6   Dorothy Osler (1998) 'The Quilt Designers of North East England' in *Uncoverings* (American Quilt Study Group, Lincoln NE) issue 19, p. 67
7   Michele Walker (1990) *The Passionate Quilter – Ideas and Techniques from Leading Quilters*. Ebury Press, London, p. 16

Hexagon Quilt

1   Dinah Travis (1995) 'Patterns in Abundance' in *Quilt Treasures – The Quilters' Guild Heritage Search*. Deirdre McDonald Books, London, p. 37
2   Janine Jannière (2003) *Mosaïques d'étoffes à la recherche de l'hexagone*. Normandy Musée des Traditions et Arts Normands et Musée Industriel de la Corderie, Vallois

3   Bridget Long (2003) 'A Comparative Study of the 1718 Silk Patchwork Coverlet' in *Quilt Studies* (British Quilt Study Group, Halifax) issue 4/5, p. 63
4   Deryn O'Connor (2001) 'Object of Desire: Mary Prince Quilt Top' in *The Quilter* (The Quilters' Guild of the British Isles, Halifax) issue 88, p. 9

Mosaic Quilt

1   Laurel Horton (2002) *An Elegant Geometry: Tradition, Migration and Variation in Mosaic Quilts Paper Template Piecing in the South Carolina Low Country*. Curious Works Press, Greenville and Charleston Museum, p. 14
2   Virginia Gunn (1983) 'Victorian Silk Template Patchwork in American Periodicals 1850–1875' in *Uncoverings* (American Quilt Study Group, Lincoln NE) issue 4, pp. 9–25

Strippy Quilt

1   Dorothy Osler (1999) 'The Classic Strippy Quilt: Its Origins and Development' in *Quilt Studies* (British Quilt Study Group, Halifax) issue 1, p. 10
2   Ibid, p. 17
3   Pauline Adams and Bridget Long (1995) 'Traditions of Quilting' in *Quilt Treasures*. Deirdre McDonald Books, London, p. 81
4   Dorothy Osler (1999) 'The Classic Strippy Quilt: Its Origins and Development' in *Quilt Studies* (British Quilt Study Group, Halifax) issue 1, p. 9
5   Jonathan Holstein (1971) *The Pieced Quilt: A North American Tradition*. McClelland and Stewart, Toronto, p. 73
6   Florence H Pettit (1974) *America's Indigo Blues Resist-Printed and Dyed Textiles of the Eighteenth Century*. Hastings House, New York, p. 110

Appliqué Quilt

1   Bridget Long (2001) 'A Study of a Late Nineteenth Century Appliqué Coverlet' in *Quilt Studies* (British Quilt Study Group, Halifax) issue 3, p. 33
2   Ibid, p. 36

ACKNOWLEDGMENTS

The Quilters' Guild appreciates the skill, experience and time given by the 12 outstanding quilters who have contributed to this book: Annette Morgan, Jo Rednall, Dinah Travis, Hilary Richardson, Judy Fairless, Linda Kemshall, Sheena Norquay, Davina Thomas, Barbara Weeks, Laura Kemshall, Melyn Robinson and Janice Gunner.

Much of the work done for The Quilters' Guild is voluntary and The Quilters' Guild wishes to thank the following members for all their help, advice and support during the production of this book: Judy Fairless, Rachel Nichols, Janet Rae, Judith Barker, Freda Moody, Linda Durant, Margaret Rayner, Carolyn Ferguson and Tina Fenwick Smith.

The Quilters' Guild staff at Dean Clough, Halifax have been very supportive throughout the whole project and thanks go to: Jane Fellows (Administrator), Rachel Terry (Curator), Christine Whitehouse (Library Assistant) and Isobel Holland (Outreach Worker).

The Quilters' Guild wishes to acknowledge the help and advice provided by Vivienne Wells and all the editing, design and photographic staff at David & Charles.

BIBLIOGRAPHY

The following books are recommended by the quilters featured in this book.

Deirdre Amsden (1994) *Colourwash Quilts: A Personal Approach to Design and Technique*. That Patchwork Place, Bothell WA [Red and White Quilt]

Jan Beaney (1998) *The Art of the Needle: Designing in Fabric and Thread*. Century Hutchinson, London [Appliqué Quilt]

Jan Beaney and Jean Littlejohn (1991) *A Complete Guide to Creative Embroidery: Designs, Textures, Stitches*. Century Editions, London [Hexagon Quilt]

Caryl Bryer Fallert (1996) *A Spectrum of Quilts 1983–1995*. American Quilters' Society, Paducah KY [Frame Quilt]

Pauline Burbidge (2000) *Quilt Studio: Innovative Techniques for Confident and Creative Quiltmaking and Design*. The Quilt Digest Press, Chicago IL [Mosaic Quilt; Appliqué Quilt]

Valerie Campbell-Harding (1983) *Strip Patchwork*. Batsford, London [Mosaic Quilt]

Valerie Campbell-Harding (1990) *Fabric Painting for Embroidery*. Batsford, London [Frame Quilt; Quilt with a Message]

Erika Carter (1996) *Personal Imagery in Art Quilts*. Fiber Studio Press, Seattle WA [Crazy Quilt]

Nancy Crow (1990) *Quilts and Influences*. American Quilters' Society, Paducah KY [Crazy Quilt]

Bailey Curtis (2001) *Dyeing to Colour*. Bailey Curtis, 10 Corsend Road, Hartpury GL19 3BP, UK [Frame Quilt]

Maurice de Sausmarez (1964) *Basic Design: The Dynamics of Visual Form*. Studio Vista, London [Red and White Quilt]

Jane Dunnewold (1996) *Complex Cloth*. That Patchwork Place, Bothell WA [Quilt with a Message; Mosaic Quilt]

Harriet Hargrave (1995) *Heirloom Machine Quilting*. C&T Publishing 1995, Lafayette CA [Red and White Quilt]

Barbara Hewitt (1995) *Blueprints on Fabric*. Interweave Press, Loveland CO [Quilt with a Message]

Judy Hopkins (1989) *One of a Kind Quilts*. That Patchwork Place, Bothell WA [Wholecloth Quilt]

Ruth Issett (1998) *Colour on Fabric and Paper*. Batsford, London [Frame Quilt]

Ruth Issett (2001) *Glorious Papers*. Batsford, London [Frame Quilt]

Michael James (1998) *Art and Inspiration*. C&T Publishing, Lafayette CA [Crazy Quilt]

Karin Jerstorp and Eva Köhlmark (1988) *The Textile Design Book: Understanding and Creating Pattern Using Texture, Space and Colour*. A&C Black, London [Wholecloth Quilt; Hexagon Quilt]

Ann Johnston (1997) *Colour By Accident: Low-Water Immersion Dyeing*. Ann Johnston, Ashland OH [Crazy Quilt]

Ann Johnston (2000) *The Quilters' Book of Design*. Quilt Digest Press, Chicago IL [Wholecloth Quilt]

Ann Johnston (2001) *Colour by Design: Paint and Print with Dye*. Ann Johnston, Ashland OH [Crazy Quilt]

Sherrill Kahn (2001) *Creating with Paint: New Ways, New Materials*. Martingale and Co, Seattle WA [Frame Quilt]

Jean Ray Laury (1992) *Imagery on Fabric*. C&T Publishing, Lafayette CA [Quilt with a Message]

Mickey Lawler (1999) *Sky Dyes*. C&T Publishing, Lafayette CA [Appliqué Quilt]

Libby Lehman (1997) *Threadplay*. That Patchwork Place, Bothell WA [Mosaic Quilt]

Ruth B McDowell (1996) *Art and Inspirations*. C&T Publishing, Lafayette CA [Frame Quilt]

Ruth B McDowell (1998) *Piecing – Expanding the Basics*. C&T Publishing, Lafayette CA [Red and White Quilt]

Gwen Marston and Joe Cunningham (1993) *Quilting with Style – Principles for Great Pattern Design*. American Quilters' Society, Paducah KY [Wholecloth Quilt]

Sandra Meech (2003) *Contemporary Quilt Design, Surface and Stitch*. Batsford, London [Appliqué Quilt]

Jan Messent (1988) *The Embroiderer's Workbook*. Batsford, London [Hexagon Quilt]

Jan Messent (1992) *Design Sources for Pattern*. Crochet Design, Morecombe [Hexagon Quilt]

Jan Messent (1992) *Designing with Pattern*. Crochet Design, Morecombe [Cord-Quilted Cushion; Hexagon Quilt; Mosaic Quilt]

Jan Messent (1998) *Designing with Motifs and Borders*. Madeira Threads, Thirsk [Cord-Quilted Cushion; Mosaic Quilt]

Maurine Noble, Elizabeth Hendricks and Ursula Reikes (1998) *Machine Quilting with Decorative Threads*. Martingale and Co, Seattle WA [Wholecloth Quilt]

Katie Pasquini Masopust (1996) *Fractured Landscape Quilts*. C&T Publishing, Lafayette CA [Red and White Quilt]

Chris Rich (1993) *The Book of Paper Cutting: A Complete Guide to all the Techniques*. Sterling Publishing, New York [Red and White Quilt]

Deirdre Scherer (1998) *Work in Fabric and Thread*. C&T Publishing, Lafayette CA [Red and White Quilt]

Elly Sienkiewicz (1989) *Baltimore Beauties and Beyond* (Volume 1). C&T Publishing, Lafayette CA [Broderie Perse Bags]

Willow Ann Soltow (1993) *Designing Your Own Quilts*. Chilton Book Co, Radnor PA [Wholecloth Quilt]

Joen Wolfrom (1995) *The Visual Dance – Creating Spectacular Quilts*. C&T Publishing, Lafayette CA [Wholecloth Quilt]

General How-To Books

Susan Denton and Barbara Macey (1987) *Quiltmaking*. David & Charles, Newton Abbot

Katharine Guerrier (2004) *Quilting from Start to Finish: The Complete Guide to Machine and Hand Quilting*. David & Charles, Newton Abbot

Linda Seward (1987) *The Complete Book of Patchwork, Quilting and Appliqué*. Mitchell Beazley, London

Michelle Walker (1987) *The Complete Book of Quiltmaking*. Ebury Press, London

SUPPLIERS

The following products and suppliers are recommended by the quilters featured in this book.

Art Van Go
16 Hollybush Lane, Datchworth, Hertfordshire SG3 6RE, UK
Tel: 01438 814946 Fax: 01438 816267
For art supplies, dyes, fabric paints and printing inks
(Red and White Quilt)

Barnyarns
Brickyard Road, Boroughbridge, North Yorkshire YO51 9NS, UK
Tel: 0870 870 8586 Fax: 01423 326 221
Email: techsup@barnyarns.com
For embroidery and quilting threads (Red and White Quilt; Wholecloth Quilt)

CottonPatch
1285 Stratford Road, Hallgreen, Birmingham B28 9AJ, UK
Tel: 0121 702 2840 Fax: 0121 778 5924
Email: mailorder@cottonpatch.net
For fabric and quilting supplies (Red and White Quilt)

European Trimmings Corporation
Enterprise House, 94 David Street, Bridgeton, Glasgow, UK
Tel: 0141 550 1188 Fax: 0141 550 2999
Email: sales@etc-embroidery.co.uk
For tear-away stabilizer (Mosaic Quilt)

Inca Studio
10 Duke Street, Princes Risborough, Buckinghamshire
HP27 0AT, UK
Tel: 01844 343343 Fax: 01844 201 263
Email: mail@incastudio.com
For threads (Appliqué Quilt)

Kemtex Educational Supplies
Chorley Business and Technology Centre, Euxton Lane, Chorley,
Lancashire PR76TE, UK
Tel: 01257 230220 Fax: 01257 230225
For fabric dyes (Strippy Quilt; Quilt with a Message; Crazy Quilt;
Appliqué Quilt)

MH Textiles
Churchover, Rugby, Warwickshire CV23 0EW, UK
Tel: 01788 833102
Email: enquiries@mhtextiles.co.uk
For chamois leather (Cord-Quilted Cushion)

Omega Dyes
Tippet's Cottage, Kenwyn Church Road, Truro, Cornwall TR1 3DR, UK
Tel & Fax: 01308 485242
Email: lindsay@omegadyes.fsnet.co.uk
For dyes including Synthapol and Dyrect Dyes (Frame Quilt)

The Quilt Room
20 West Street, Dorking, Surrey RH4 1BL, UK
Tel: 01306 877307 Fax: 01306 877407
Email: sales@quiltroom.co.uk
For fabric and quilting supplies (Red and White Quilt)

Rainbow Silks
6 Wheeler's Yard, High Street, Great Missenden, Buckinghamshire
HP16 0AL, UK
Tel: 01494 862111 Fax: 01494 862651
Email: caroline@rainbowsilks.co.uk
For fabric paints, silks, dyes and surface decorations (Mosaic Quilt)

Rio Designs
Flint Cottage, Treacle Lane, Rushden, Buntingford, Hertfordshire
SG9 0SL, UK
Tel & Fax: 01763 288234
Email: sales@riodesigns.co.uk
For computer software and consumables including Bubble Jet Set 2000,
Quilt Pro and freezer paper (Quilt with a Message; Hexagon Quilt)

The Silk Route
Cross Cottage, Cross Lane, Frimley Green, Surrey GU16 6LN, UK
Tel: 01252 835781
Email: hilary@thesilkroute.co.uk
For silk and luxury fabrics (Wholecloth Quilt)

Silverprint
12 Valentine Place, London, SE1 8QH, UK
Tel: 0207 620 0844 Fax: 020 7620 0129
Email: sales@silverprint.co.uk
For chemicals for cyanotypes (Quilt with a Message)

The Software Centre
PO 2000, Nottingham, Nottinghamshire NG11 7GW, UK
Tel: 0115 914 2000 Fax: 0115 914 2020
For computer software including Serif DrawPlus,
Serif PhotoPlus and Serif PagePlus (Hexagon Quilt)

Whaleys (Bradford) Ltd
Harris Court, Great Horton, Bradford, West Yorkshire BD7 4EQ, UK
Tel: 01274 576718 Fax: 01274 521309
Email: whaleys@btinternet.com
For fabric (Strippy Quilt; Crazy Quilt; Wholecloth Quilt; Mosaic Quilt;
Log Cabin Quilt)

Wolfin Textiles Ltd
359 Uxbridge Road, Hatch End, Middlesex HA5 4JN, UK
Tel: 0208 428 9555 Fax: 0208 428 9955
Email: cotton@wolfintextiles.co.uk
For silk and silk-mix fabrics (Mosaic Quilt; Appliqué Quilt)

ABOUT THE QUILTERS' GUILD

The Quilters' Guild of the British Isles is a national educational charity with over 7000 members. Membership is available to anyone with an interest in quilts or quiltmaking. There are membership categories for overseas, associates, students and young quilters. The Quilters' Guild has a number of specialist interest groups: the British Quilt Study Group, Miniature Quilt Group and Contemporary Quilt Group, each with an additional annual subscription.

The Quilters' Guild of the British Isles, Room 190, Dean Clough, Halifax, West Yorkshire HX3 5AX.
Tel: 01422 347 669
Email: info@qghalifax.org.uk
Website: www.quiltersguild.org.uk

ABOUT BRIDGET LONG

Bridget Long is a former Heritage Officer and President of The Quilters' Guild of the British Isles. She currently acts as advisor to the Guild's Acquisitions committee and also serves on the Advisory Board of the International Quilt Study Center based at the University of Nebraska-Lincoln, USA.

A quilt historian, textile collector, lecturer and author, Bridget was an examiner for the Quilters' Guild British Quilt Heritage Project in the early 1990s. She contributed to the resultant book *Quilt Treasures: The Quilters' Guild Heritage Search* (Deirdre McDonald Books, London 1995). Since the conclusion of that three-year project she has pursued quilt research and, as an active member of the British Quilt Study Group, has published research papers in the journal *Quilt Studies*.

Also an experienced quiltmaker, Bridget was one of the first to qualify in the City and Guilds Patchwork and Quilting course in the early 1990s.

INDEX